PASTA & PIZZA

PASTA & PIZZA

CARLA CAPALBO

photographs by
AMANDA HEYWOOD

Sebastian Kelly

This edition published in 1998
by SEBASTIAN KELLY

Produced by Anness Publishing Limited
Hermes House, 88-89 Blackfriars Road,
London SE1 8HA

ISBN 1 901688 48 8

Publisher: Joanna Lorenz
Project Editor: Lindsay Porter
Designers: Patrick McLeavey and Jo Brewer
Photographer: Amanda Heywood
Prop Styling: Amanda Heywood, Carla Capalbo
Home Economist: Carla Capalbo
Assistant Home Economists: Marilyn Forbes, Beverly Le Blanc, Wallace Heim

A CIP catalogue record for this book is available from the British Library

Originally published as part of a larger compendium, *The Ultimate Italian Cookbook*

Printed in Singapore by Star Standard Industries Pte. Ltd.

10 9 8 7 6 5 4 3 2 1

MEASUREMENTS

Three sets of measurements have been provided in the recipes, in the following order: Metric, Imperial and American. It is essential that units of measurement are not mixed within each recipe. Where conversions result in awkward numbers, these have been rounded for convenience but are still accurate enough for successful results.

CONTENTS

Introduction

Italy is a country of great diversity. Its long Mediterranean coastline encloses a landscape of fertile plains, forest-covered mountains and arid rocks. From the hot, dry south to the cool Alpine foothills, the climate varies markedly. So do the local crops: rice, maize and ham are northern staples, while olives, durum wheat and tomatoes thrive in the southern heat.

Despite the advent of industrialization and mass-marketing, traditional foods are still central to the cultural identity of each region. This is partly due to the way in which recipes are learned: orally passed from generation to generation, and rarely written down in cookbooks, they survive in families for years with little or no changes made to them.

A great deal of Italian food comes from this *contadino*, or peasant heritage and pizzas and pasta dishes are undoubtedly among the most popular. Most of these recipes can be prepared quickly and economically. Delicious pizza toppings can be assembled in next to no time from basic store cupboard ingredients, and aromatic sauces can be created in the time it takes pasta to boil.

In addition, these dishes are generally high in vegetables and carbohydrates and low in animal fat – providing the perfect solution for today's more health conscious life-styles without sacrificing flavour.

Fresh Produce

Italian cooking is based on the creative use of fresh, seasonal ingredients. Vegetables and herbs play central roles in almost every aspect of the menu. In the markets, there is a sense of anticipation at the beginning of each new season, heralded by the arrival, on the beautifully displayed stalls, of the year's first artichokes, olives, chestnuts or wild mushrooms. Seasonal recipes come to the fore and make the most of available produce.

Many of the vegetables once considered exotically Mediterranean are now readily available in the markets and supermarkets of most countries. Fennel and aubergine, peppers, courgettes and radicchio are now increasingly present in pasta sauces and pizzas.

Wherever you shop, look for the freshest possible fruits and vegetables. Choose unblemished, firm, sun-ripened produce, preferably locally or organically grown. Fresh herbs like basil, parsley and sage are easy to cultivate in window boxes and gardens and have an infinitely finer flavour than their dried counterparts. Italian cuisine is not a complicated or sophisticated style of cooking, but your recipes will benefit immeasurably by starting with the best quality ingredients you can find.

Below: ***Italian cuisine does not rely on unusual produce, but it must be as fresh as possible.***

Store Cupboard Ingredients

Perhaps the single most important ingredient in a modern Italian kitchen is olive oil. The fruity flavour of a fine extra-virgin olive oil perfumes any dish it is used in, from pesto sauce to the simplest salad dressing. Buy the best olive oil you can afford: one bottle goes a long way and makes a huge difference to any recipe.

Balsamic vinegar has only recently become widely available outside of Italy. Made by the slow wood-aging process of wine vinegar, the finest varieties are deliciously mellow and fragrant. The taste is quite sweet and concentrated, so only a little is needed.

Porcini mushrooms are found in the woods in various parts of Europe in autumn. They can be eaten cooked fresh, or sliced thinly and dried in the sun or in special ovens. A few dried porcini soaked in water adds a deliciously woodsy flavour to sauces and pizzas.

Olives are one of Italy's most wonderful native ingredients. Unfortunately, freshly cured olives do not travel very well, and many of the most delicious varieties are not available outside the Mediterranean. Sample canned or bottled olives before adding them to sauces as they sometimes acquire an unpleasant metallic taste that could spoil the flavour of the dish.

A typical Italian store cupboard also contains a supply of dried, natural ingredients. Dried beans and lentils are stored in air-tight dispensers for use in soups.

Capers, pine nuts, sun-dried tomatoes, dried chillies, juniper berries and fennel seeds are some of the other ingredients commonly used to give Italian dishes their characteristic flavours, and are good basics to keep in the store cupboard.

Above: *An Italian kitchen might have a selection of dried beans, pulses and rice; olives, olive oil and good quality vinegar; as well as dried spices and other flavourings.*

Meats and Cheeses

Cured meats and cheeses make wonderful pizza toppings or additions to pasta sauces, or can be assembled for a quick, authentic antipasto. A popular antipasto consists of a plate of mixed prepared meats and sausages. Salamis, pancetta, air-dried bresaola, coppa and mortadella sausages are some of the meats most commonly used in Italy, often served with an accompaniment of crusty bread and butter. Prosciutto crudo, raw Parma ham, is the most prized of all meats.

An Italian meal is more likely to end with a selection of cheeses and fruit than a sweet dessert. Among the huge variety of cheeses, the following are some of the best known:

Gorgonzola is made in Lombardy and is a creamy blue cheese. It has a mild flavour when young, which becomes stronger with maturity.

Mascarpone is a rich, triple-cream cheese with a mild flavour. It is often used in desserts as a substitute for whipped cream.

Mozzarella is a fresh, white cheese made from water buffalo's, or, more commonly, cow's milk. The texture is soft and chewy and the taste mild.

Parmesan is a long-aged, full-flavoured cheese with a hard rind, used for both grating and eating in slivers. The large wheels are aged from 18–36 months. Fresh Parmesan is superb, and is incomparably better than the ready-grated varieties.

Pecorino is made from ewe's milk, and comes in two main types, Pecorino Romano and Pecorino Tuscano. This salted, sharp-flavoured cheese is widely used for dessert eating, and for grating when mature.

Scamorza is made from cow's milk. Its distinctive shape is due to being hung from a string during aging.

Below: *A typical Italian meal might include cured meat as an antipasto, and finish with cheese instead of a sweet dessert.*

Equipment

1 *Earthenware pot*. Excellent for slow-cooking stews, soups or sauces. Can be used either in the oven or on top of the stove with a metal heat diffuser under it to discourage cracking. Many shapes and sizes are available. To season a terracotta pot before using it for the first time, immerse in cold water overnight. Remove from the water and rub the unglazed bottom with garlic. Fill with water and bring slowly to the boil. Discard the water. Repeat, changing the water, until the 'earth' taste disappears.

2 *Pasta rolling pin*. A length of dowelling 5 cm/2 in in diameter can also be used. Smooth with sandpaper before using for the first time.

3 *Pestle and mortar*. For hand-grinding spices, pepper, herbs and breadcrumbs.

4 *Hand food mill*. Excellent for soups, sauces and tomato 'passata': the pulp passes through the holes leaving the seeds and skin behind.

5 *Colander*. Indispensable for draining hot pasta and vegetables.

6 *Parmesan cheese knife*. In Italy Parmesan is not cut with a conventional knife, but broken off the large cheese wheels using this kind of wedge. Insert the point and apply pressure.

7 *Pizza cutting wheel*. Useful for cutting slices, although a sharp knife may also be used.

8 *Palette knife*. Very useful for spreading and smoothing.

9 *Spaghetti spoon*. The wooden 'teeth' catch the spaghetti strands as they boil.

10 *Meat hammer*. For pounding escalopes. Also useful for crushing nuts and spices.

11 *Pasta machine*. Many are available, including electric and industrial models. Most have an adjustable roller width and thin and wide noodle cutters.

12 *Icing nozzles*. For piping decorations, garnishes, etc. Use with a nylon or paper pastry bag.

13 *Wide vegetable peeler*. Very easy to use for all sizes of vegetable.

14 *Italian gelato scoop*. Good for soft ices that are not too solid.

15 *Ice cream scoop*. Better for firm and well-frozen ice creams.

16 *Olive stoner*. Can also be used for pitting cherries.

17 *Whisk*. Excellent for smoothing sauces, beating egg whites.

18 *Fluted pastry cutter*. For cutting fresh pasta or pastry.

19 *Biscuit cutter*. Also used for cutting fresh pasta shapes.

Pasta

Dried and home-made egg pastas are easy to prepare and the varied shapes are always family favourites. Nutritious fresh sauces made from vegetables, fish, meat and cheese offer endless possibilities for first and main courses.

How to Make Egg Pasta by Hand

This classic recipe for egg noodles from Emilia-Romagna calls for just three ingredients: flour and eggs, with a little salt. In other regions of Italy water, milk or oil are sometimes added. Use plain or strong white flour, and large eggs. As a general guide, use 70 g/2½ oz/½ cup of flour to each egg. Quantities will vary with the exact size of the eggs.

To serve 3–4
2 eggs, salt
140 g/5 oz/1 cup flour

To serve 4–6
3 eggs, salt
210 g/7½ oz/1½ cups flour

To serve 6–8
4 eggs, salt
280 g/10 oz/2 cups flour

1 ▲ Place the flour in the centre of a clean smooth work surface. Make a well in the middle. Break the eggs into the well. Add a pinch of salt.

2 Start beating the eggs with a fork, gradually drawing the flour from the inside walls of the well. As the paste thickens, continue the mixing with your hands. Incorporate as much flour as possible until the mixture forms a mass. It will still be lumpy. If it still sticks to your hands, add a little more flour. Set the dough aside. Scrape off all traces of the dough from the work surface until it is perfectly smooth. Wash and dry your hands.

About Pasta

Most pasta is made from durum wheat flour and water – durum is a special kind of wheat with a very high protein content. Egg pasta, *pasta all'uova*, contains flour and eggs, and is used for flat noodles such as tagliatelle, or for lasagne. Very little wholewheat pasta is eaten in Italy, but it is quite popular in other countries.

All these types of pasta are available dried in packets, and will keep almost indefinitely. Fresh pasta is now more widely available and can be bought in most supermarkets. It can be very good, but can never compare to home-made egg pasta.

Pasta comes in countless shapes and sizes. It is very difficult to give a definite list, as the names for the shapes vary from country to country. In some cases, just within Italy, the same shape can appear with several different names, depending upon which region it is in. The pasta shapes called for in this book, as well as many others, are illustrated in the introduction. The most common names have been listed.

Most of the recipes in this book specify the pasta shape most appropriate for a particular sauce. They can, of course, be replaced with another kind. A general rule is that long pasta goes better with tomato or thinner sauces, while short pasta is best for chunkier, meatier sauces. But this rule should not be followed too rigidly. Part of the fun of cooking and eating pasta is in the endless combinations of sauce and pasta shapes.

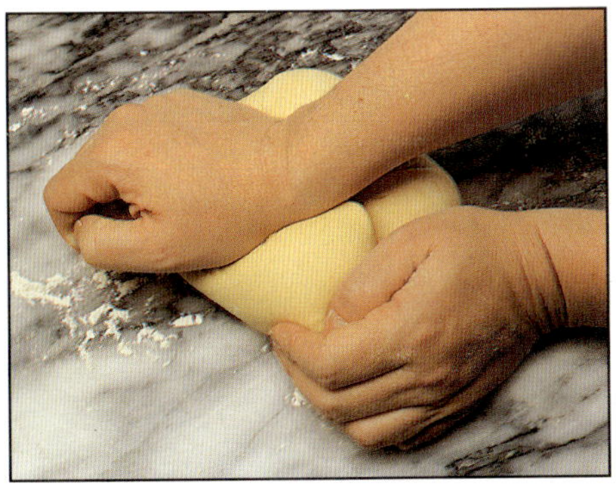

3 ▲ Lightly flour the work surface. Knead the dough by pressing it away from you with the heel of your hands, and then folding it over towards you. Repeat this action over and over, turning the dough as you knead. Work for about 10 minutes, or until the dough is smooth and elastic.

4 ▲ If you are using more than 2 eggs, divide the dough in half. Flour the rolling pin and the work surface. Pat the dough into a disc and begin rolling it out into a flat circle, rotating it one quarter turn after each roll to keep its shape round. Roll until the disc is about 3 mm/⅛ in thick.

5 ▲ Roll out the dough until it is paper-thin by rolling up onto the rolling pin and simultaneously giving a sideways stretching with the hands. Wrap the near edge of the dough around the centre of the rolling pin, and begin rolling the dough up away from you. As you roll back and forth, slide your hands from the centre towards the outer edges of the pin, stretching and thinning out the pasta.

6 ▲ Quickly repeat these movements until about two-thirds of the sheet of pasta is wrapped around the pin. Lift and turn the wrapped pasta sheet about 45° before unrolling it. Repeat the rolling and stretching process, starting from a new point of the sheet each time to keep it evenly thin. By the end (this process should not last more than 8 to 10 minutes or the dough will lose its elasticity) the whole sheet should be smooth and almost transparent. If the dough is still sticky, lightly flour your hands as you continue rolling and stretching.

7 ▲ If you are making noodles (tagliatelle, fettuccine etc.) lay a clean dish towel on a table or other flat surface, and unroll the pasta sheet on it, letting about a third of the sheet hang over the edge of the table. Rotate the dough every 10 minutes. Roll out the second sheet of dough if you are using more than 2 eggs. After 25–30 minutes the pasta will have dried enough to cut. Do not overdry or the pasta will crack as it is cut.

8 ▲ To cut tagliatelle, fettuccine or tagliolini, fold the sheet of pasta into a flat roll about 10 cm/4 in wide. Cut across the roll to form noodles of the desired width. Tagliolini is 3 mm/⅛ in; Fettuccine is 4 mm/⅙ in; Tagliatelle is 6 mm/¼ in. After cutting, open out the noodles, and let them dry for about 5 minutes before cooking. These noodles may be stored for some weeks without refrigeration. Allow the noodles to dry completely before storing them, uncovered, in a dry cupboard, and use as required.

9 ▲ To cut the pasta for lasagne or pappardelle, do not fold or dry the rolled out dough. Lasagne is made from rectangles approximately 13 cm/5 in by 9 cm/3½ in. Pappardelle are large noodles cut with a fluted pastry wheel. They are about 2 cm/¾ in wide.

Egg Pasta Made by Machine

Making pasta with a machine is quick and easy. The results are perhaps not quite as fine as with handmade pasta, but they are certainly better than store-bought pastas.

You will need a pasta-making machine, either hand-cranked or electric. Use the same proportions of eggs, flours and salt as for Handmade Egg Pasta.

1 ▲ Place the flour in the centre of a clean smooth work surface. Make a well in the middle. Break the eggs into the well. Add a pinch of salt. Start beating the eggs with a fork, gradually drawing the flour from the inside walls of the well. As the paste thickens, continue mixing with your hands. Incorporate as much flour as possible until the mixture forms a mass. It will still be lumpy. If it sticks to your hands, add a little more flour. Set the dough aside and scrape the work surface clean.

2 ▲ Set the machine rollers at their widest (kneading) setting. Pull off a piece of dough the size of a small orange. Place the remaining dough between two soup plates. Feed the dough through the rollers. Fold it in half, end to end, and feed it through again 7 or 8 times, turning it and folding it over after each kneading. The dough should be smooth and fairly evenly rectangular. If it sticks to the machine, brush with flour. Lay it out on a lightly floured work surface or on a clean dish towel, and repeat with the remaining dough, broken into pieces the same size.

3 ▲ Adjust the machine to the next line setting. Feed each strip through once only, and replace on the drying surface. Keep them in the order in which they were first kneaded.

4 ▲ Reset the machine to the next setting. Repeat, passing each strip through once. Repeat for each remaining roller setting until the pasta is the right thickness – for most purposes this is given by the next to last setting, except for very delicate strips such as tagliolini, or for ravioli. If the pasta strips get too long, cut them in half to facilitate handling.

5 ▲ When all the strips are the desired thickness they may be machine-cut into noodles, or hand-cut for lasagne or pappardelle, as described for handmade pasta earlier. When making noodles, be sure the pasta is fairly dry, but not brittle, or the noodles may stick together when cut. Select the desired width of cutter, and feed the strips through.

6 Separate the noodles, and leave to dry for at least 15 minutes before using. They may be stored for some weeks without refrigeration. Allow them to dry completely before storing them, uncovered, in a dry cupboard. They may also be frozen, first loose on trays and then packed together.

7 If you are making stuffed pasta (ravioli, cannelloni etc.) do not let the pasta strips dry out before filling them, but proceed immediately with the individual recipes.

~ PASTA VERDE ~

Follow the same recipe, adding 50 g/2 oz/¼ cup cooked, very finely chopped spinach (after having been squeezed very dry) to the eggs and flour. You may have to add a little more flour to absorb the moisture from the spinach. This pasta is very suitable for stuffed recipes, as it seals better than plain egg pasta.

How to Cook Dried Pasta

Store-bought and home-made pasta are cooked in the same way, though the timings vary greatly. Home-made pasta cooks virtually in the time it takes for the water to return to the boil after it is put in.

1 Always cook pasta in a large amount of rapidly boiling water. Use at least 1 litre/2 pints/5 cups of water to each 115 g/4 oz/½ cup pasta.

2 ▲ The water should be salted at least 2 minutes before the pasta is added, to give the salt time to dissolve. Add about 20 g/1½ tbsp salt per 450 g/1 lb/pasta. You may want to vary the saltiness of the cooking water.

3 ▲ Drop the pasta into the boiling water all at once. Use a wooden spoon to help ease long pasta in as it softens, to prevent it from breaking. Stir frequently to prevent the pasta sticking to itself or to the pan. Cook the pasta at a fast boil, but be prepared to lower the heat if it boils over.

4 Timing is critical in pasta cooking. Follow packet indications for store-bought pasta, but it is best in all cases to test for doneness by tasting, several times if necessary. In Italy pasta is always eaten *al dente*, which mens firm to the bite. Cooked this way it is just tender, but its "soul" (the innermost part) is still firm. Overcooked pasta will be mushy.

5 ▲ Place a colander in the sink before the pasta has finished cooking. As soon as the pasta tastes done, tip it all into the colander (you may first want to reserve a cupful of the hot cooking water to add to the sauce if it needs thinning). Shake the colander lightly to remove most but not all of the cooking water. Pasta should never be over-drained.

6 ▲ Quickly turn the pasta into a warmed serving dish, and immediately toss it with a little butter or oil, or the prepared sauce. Alternatively, turn it into the cooking pan with the sauce, where it will be cooked for 1–2 minutes more as it is mixed into the sauce. Never allow pasta to sit undressed, as it will stick together and become unpalatable.

How to Cook Egg Pasta

Fresh egg pasta, especially home-made, cooks very much faster than dried pasta. Make sure everything is ready (the sauce, serving dishes, etc.) before you start boiling egg pasta, as there will not be time once the cooking starts, and egg pasta becomes soft and mushy very quickly.

1 Always cook pasta in a large amount of rapidly boiling water. Use at least litre/2 pints/5 cups of water to a quantity of pasta made with 115 g/4 oz/1 cup of flour. Salt the water as for dried pasta.

2 ▲ Drop the pasta into the boiling water all at once. Stir gently to prevent the pasta sticking to itself or to the pan. Cook the pasta at a fast boil.

3 ▲ Freshly made pasta can be done as little as 15 seconds after the cooking water comes back to the boil. Stuffed pasta takes a few minutes longer. When done, tip the pasta into the colander and proceed as for dried pasta.

Pasta

Pasta in its many forms is a staple of Italian cuisine. These are just some of the varieties available.

1 *Alfabeto.* Small alphabet pasta for soups.

2 *Anellini.* Little rings used in soups and broth.

3 *Canneroni.* Pasta rings for thick vegetable soups.

4 *Capellini.* Very fine "angel hair" pasta, can be broken up and used in broths.

5 *Chifferi piccoli lisci.* Smooth, macaroni-like pasta used in baked dishes.

6 *Chifferi piccoli rigati.* Ridged version of the above.

7 *Conchigliette.* Small shells used in soups.

8 *Conchigliette rigati.* Small, ridged shells used in thick soups.

9 *Conchiglioni rigati.* Large, ridged shells used for stuffing and baking.

10 *Ditali.* Used in soups, traditionally with dried beans.

11 *Ditalini.* Soup pasta, smaller than ditali.

12 *Ditalini lisci.* Smooth ditalini, also used in soups.

13 *Elicoidali.* Good for baked dishes, or those with chunky sauces.

14 *Fagiolini.* "String beans" used in soups.

15 *Farfalle.* Butterflies or bows. Excellent with prawns and peas and in cold pasta salads.

16 *Fusilli.* These spirals are ideal with tomato and vegetable sauces.

17 *Fusilli integrali.* Wholewheat spirals. Good hot or cold with thick vegetable sauces.

18 *Fusillata casareccia.* The twisted shape is good with tomato sauce.

19 *Gnocchi.* Shells for chunky vegetable or meat sauces. Gnocchi tricolori (19a) is flavoured with tomato and spinach.

20 *Gnocchi integrali.* Wholewheat shells popular in vegetarian dishes, hot or cold.

21 *Gnocchetti sardi.* Sardinian shells. Good with lamb or fish sauces.

22 *Lasagne doppia riccia.* Frilly-edged lasagne. This is a dry version of the popular egg pasta, used for stuffed and baked dishes.

23 *Lasagne verdi.* Spinach gives this lasagne its green colour.

24 *Lingue di passero, Bavette.* Traditionally paired with the classic pesto sauce.

25 *Linguine, Bavettine.* This finer version of lingue de passoro is good with fish sauces.

26 *Lumache rigate grandi.* These large, ridged "snails" are suitable for thick sauces with strong flavours such as olives and capers. Also good for pasta salads.

27 *Macaroni.* This is the English version of Italian maccherone, most popular baked with cheese.

28 *Mafaldine.* This is often eaten with sauces made from soft cheeses, such as ricotta.

29 *Mezze penne rigate tricolori.* The pasta is tinted with tomato and spinach to produce Italy's favourite colours.

30 *Orecchiette.* Dry version of the traditionally hand-made pasta popular in the south of Italy. Cooked with green vegetables.

31 *Penne lisce.* Quills or pens. Cut diagonally to catch more sauce.

32 *Penne rigate.* Ridged quills, a favourite shape in Italy. Great with tomato sauces.

33 *Pennoni rigati.* Large ridged quills. Good for baked dishes.

34 *Peperini.* Little pasta dots to add to broth or soups.

35 *Perciatellini.* This is a hollow spaghetti. Can be used with any of the usual spaghetti sauces.

36 *Pipe rigate.* "Ridged pipes". Good for thick, chunky sauces with peas or lentils.

37 *Puntalette.* For adding to soups and broths.

38 *Rigatoni.* Often baked with meat sauces and cheeses. Mezza rigatoni (38a) are smaller in size.

39 *Ruote.* Pasta wheels, always popular with children.

40 *Spaghetti integrali.* Wholewheat version of spaghetti (40a), more popular abroad than in Italy.

41 *Spaghettini.* Finer version of spaghetti, good with delicate sauces.

42 *Stelline.* Little stars, another small soup pasta.

43 *Tagliatelle.* Dried egg noodles, good with creamy sauces.

44 *Tagliatelle verdi.* Dried spinach-flavoured egg noodles.

45 *Tomato spirals.* Specially made tomato-flavoured pasta.

46 *Tortellini.* Small dumplings, often cooked and eaten in broth.

47 *Tortelloni.* Pasta dumplings stuffed with meats or cheeses.

48 *Zite.* A long hollow pasta often used with fish or tomato sauces.

23
26
19a
16
17
44
36
9
19
39
45
6
20
33
38
43
21
5
13
38a
32
15
18
3
27
29
10
14
8
4
31
30
37
7
11
34
1
2
42
46
47

Basic Tomato Sauce

Sugo di pomodoro alla napolitana

Tomato sauce is without a doubt the most popular dressing for pasta in Italy. This sauce is best made with fresh tomatoes, but works well with canned plum tomatoes.

Ingredients
60 ml/4 tbsp olive oil
1 medium onion, very finely chopped
1 clove garlic, finely chopped
450 g/1 lb tomatoes, fresh or canned, chopped, with their juice
salt and freshly ground black pepper
a few leaves fresh basil or sprigs parsley
for 4 servings of pasta

1 Heat the oil in a medium saucepan. Add the onion, and cook over moderate heat until it is translucent, 5–8 minutes.

2 ▲ Stir in the garlic and the tomatoes with their juice (add 45 ml/3 tbsp of water if you are using fresh tomatoes). Season with salt and pepper. Add the herbs. Cook for 20–30 minutes.

3 ▲ Pass the sauce through a food mill or purée in a food processor. To serve, reheat gently, correct the seasoning and pour over the drained pasta.

Special Tomato Sauce

Sugo di pomodoro

The tomatoes in this sauce are enhanced by the addition of extra vegetables. It is good served with all types of pasta or could be served as an accompaniment to stuffed vegetables.

Ingredients
700 g/1⅔ lb tomatoes, fresh or canned, chopped
1 carrot, chopped
1 stick celery, chopped
1 medium onion, chopped
1 clove garlic, crushed
75 ml/5 tbsp olive oil
salt and freshly ground black pepper
a few leaves fresh basil or a small pinch dried oregano
for 6 servings of pasta

1 Place all the ingredients in a medium heavy saucepan, and simmer together for 30 minutes.

2 ▲ Purée the sauce in a food processor, or press through a sieve.

3 ▲ Return the sauce to the pan, correct the seasoning, and simmer again for about 15 minutes.

~ COOK'S TIP ~

This sauce may be spooned into freezer bags and frozen until required. Allow to thaw to room temperature before re-heating.

Linguine with Pesto Sauce

Linguine con pesto

Pesto originates in Liguria, where the sea breezes are said to give the local basil a particularly fine flavour. It is traditionally made with a mortar and pestle, but it is easier to make in a food processor or blender. Freeze any spare pesto in an ice cube tray.

Ingredients

65 g/2½ oz/¾ cup fresh basil leaves
3–4 cloves garlic, peeled
45 ml/3 tbsp pine nuts
½ tsp salt
75 ml/5 tbsp olive oil
50 g/2 oz/½ cup freshly grated Parmesan cheese
60 ml/4 tbsp freshly grated pecorino cheese
freshly ground black pepper
500 g/1¼ lb linguine
serves 5–6

1 ▲ Place the basil, garlic, pine nuts, salt and olive oil in a blender or food processor and process until smooth. Remove to a bowl. (If desired, the sauce may be frozen at this point, before the cheeses are added).

2 ▲ Stir in the cheeses (use all Parmesan if pecorino is not available). Taste for seasoning.

3 ▲ Cook the pasta in a large pan of rapidly boiling salted water until it is *al dente*. Just before draining it, take about 60 ml/4 tbsp of the cooking water and stir it into the sauce.

4 ▲ Drain the pasta and toss with the sauce. Serve immediately.

Bologonese Meat Sauce

Ragù alla bolognese

This great meat sauce is a speciality of Bologna. It is delicious with tagliatelle or short pastas such as penne or conchiglie as well as spaghetti, and is indispensable in baked lasagne. It keeps well in the refrigerator for several days and can also be frozen.

Ingredients
25 g/1 oz/2 tbsp butter
60 ml/4 tbsp olive oil
1 medium onion, finely chopped
25 g/1 oz/2 tbsp pancetta or unsmoked bacon, finely chopped
1 carrot, finely sliced
1 stick celery, finely sliced
1 clove garlic, finely chopped
350 g/12 oz lean minced beef
salt and freshly ground black pepper
150 ml/¼ pt/⅔ cup red wine
125 ml/4 fl oz/½ cup milk
1 × 400 g/14 oz can plum tomatoes, chopped, with their juice
1 bay leaf
¼ tsp fresh thyme leaves
for 6 servings of pasta

1 ▲ Heat the butter and oil in a heavy saucepan or earthenware pot. Add the onion, and cook over moderate heat for 3–4 minutes. Add the pancetta, and cook until the onion is translucent. Stir in the carrot, celery and garlic. Cook 3–4 minutes more.

2 Add the beef, and crumble it into the vegetables with a fork. Stir until the meat loses its red colour. Season with salt and pepper.

3 ▲ Pour in the wine, raise the heat slightly, and cook until the liquid evaporates, 3–4 minutes. Add the milk, and cook until it evaporates.

4 ▲ Stir in the tomatoes with their juice, and the herbs. Bring the sauce to the boil. Reduce the heat to low, and simmer, uncovered for 1½–2 hours, stirring occasionally. Correct the seasoning before serving.

Spaghetti with Garlic and Oil

Spaghetti con aglio e olio

This is one of the simplest and most satisfying pasta dishes of all. It is very popular throughout Italy. Use the best quality oil available for this dish.

Ingredients
400 g/14 oz spaghetti
90 ml/6 tbsp extra-virgin olive oil
3 cloves garlic, chopped
60 ml/4 tbsp chopped fresh parsley
salt and freshly ground black pepper
freshly grated Parmesan cheese, to serve (optional)
serves 4

1 Drop the spaghetti into a large pan of rapidly boiling salted water.

2 ▲ In a large frying pan heat the oil and gently sauté the garlic until it is barely golden. Do not let it brown or it will taste bitter. Stir in the parsley. Season with salt and pepper. Remove from the heat until the pasta is ready.

3 ▲ Drain the pasta when it is barely *al dente*. Tip it into the pan with the oil and garlic, and cook together for 2–3 minutes, stirring well to coat the spaghetti with the sauce. Serve at once in a warmed serving bowl, with Parmesan, if desired.

Spaghetti with Walnut Sauce

Spaghetti con salsa di noci

Like pesto, this sauce is traditionally ground in a mortar and pestle, but works just as well made in a food processor. It is also very good on tagliatelle and other noodles.

Ingredients
115 g/4 oz/1 cup walnut pieces or halves
45 ml/3 tbsp plain breadcrumbs
45 ml/3 tbsp olive or walnut oil
45 ml/3 tbsp chopped fresh parsley
1–2 cloves garlic (optional)
50 g/2 oz/¼ cup butter, at room temperature
30 ml/2 tbsp cream
salt and freshly ground black pepper
400 g/14 oz wholewheat spaghetti
freshly grated Parmesan cheese, to serve
serves 4

1 Drop the nuts into a small pan of boiling water, and cook for 1–2 minutes. Drain. Slip off the skins. Dry on paper towels. Coarsely chop and set aside about a quarter of the nuts.

2 ▲ Place the remaining nuts, the breadcrumbs, oil, parsley and garlic, if using, in a food processor or blender. Process to a paste. Remove to a bowl, and stir in the softened butter and the cream. Season with salt and pepper.

3 ▲ Cook the pasta in a large pan of rapidly boiling salted water until *al dente*. Drain, and toss with the sauce. Sprinkle with the reserved chopped nuts, and pass the Parmesan separately.

Fusilli with Peppers and Onions

Fusilli con peperoni

Peppers are characteristic of southern Italy. When grilled and peeled they have a delicious smoky flavour, and are easier to digest.

Ingredients

450 g/1 lb red and yellow peppers (about 2 large ones)
90 ml/6 tbsp olive oil
1 large red onion, thinly sliced
2 cloves garlic, minced
400 g/14 oz/4 cups fusilli or other short pasta
salt and freshly ground black pepper
45 ml/3 tbsp finely chopped fresh parsley
freshly grated Parmesan cheese, to serve
serves 4

1 ▲ Place the peppers under a hot grill and turn occasionally until they are black and blistered on all sides. Remove from the heat, place in a paper bag and leave for 5 minutes.

2 ▲ Peel the peppers. Cut them into quarters, remove the stems and seeds, and slice into thin strips. Bring a large pan of water to the boil.

3 ▲ Heat the oil in a large frying pan. Add the onion, and cook over moderate heat until it is translucent, 5–8 minutes. Stir in the garlic, and cook for 2 minutes more.

4 ▲ Add salt and the pasta to the boiling water, and cook until the pasta is *al dente*.

~ COOK'S TIP ~

Peppers belong to the *capsicum annum* family. They were brought to Europe by Columbus who discovered them in Haiti. The large red, yellow and orange peppers are usually sweeter than the green varieties, and have a fuller flavour.

5 ▲ Meanwhile, add the peppers to the onions, and mix together gently. Stir in about 45 ml/3 tbsp of the pasta cooking water. Season with salt and pepper. Stir in the parsley.

6 ▲ Drain the pasta. Tip it into the pan with the vegetables, and cook over moderate heat for 3–4 minutes, stirring constantly to mix the pasta into the sauce. Serve with the Parmesan passed separately.

Orecchiette with Broccoli

Pasta e broccoli

Puglia, in southern Italy, specializes in imaginative pasta and vegetable combinations. Using the broccoli cooking water for boiling the pasta gives it more of the vegetable's flavour.

Ingredients
800 g/1¾ lb broccoli
450 g/1 lb orecchiette or penne
90 ml/6 tbsp olive oil
3 cloves garlic, finely chopped
6 anchovy fillets in oil
salt and freshly ground black pepper
serves 6

1 Peel the stems of the broccoli, starting from the base and pulling up towards the florets with a knife. Discard the woody parts of the stem. Cut florets and stems into 5 cm/2 in pieces.

2 ▲ Bring a large pan of water to the boil. Drop in the broccoli, and boil until barely tender, about 5–8 minutes. Remove the broccoli pieces from the pan to a serving bowl. Do not discard the cooking water.

3 ▲ Add salt to the broccoli cooking water. Bring it back to the boil. Drop in the pasta, stir well, and cook until it is *al dente*.

4 ▲ While the pasta is boiling, heat the oil in a small frying pan. Add the garlic and, after 2–3 minutes, the anchovy fillets. Using a fork, mash the anchovies and garlic to a paste. Cook for 3–4 minutes more.

5 ▲ Before draining the pasta, ladle 1–2 cupfuls of the cooking water over the broccoli. Add the drained pasta and the hot anchovy and oil mixture. Mix well, and season with salt and pepper if necessary. Serve at once.

Spaghetti with Eggs and Bacon

Spaghetti alla carbonara

One of the classic pasta sauces, about which a debate remains: whether or not it should contain cream. Purists believe that it should not.

Ingredients
30 ml/2 tbsp olive oil
150 g/5 oz/generous ½ cup bacon, cut into matchsticks
1 clove garlic, crushed
400 g/14 oz spaghetti
3 eggs, at room temperature
75 g/3 oz/¾ cup freshly grated Parmesan cheese
salt and freshly ground black pepper
serves 4

1 ▲ Bring a large pan of water to the boil. In a medium frying pan, heat the oil and sauté the bacon and the garlic until the bacon renders its fat and starts to brown. Remove and discard the garlic. Keep the bacon and its fat hot until needed.

2 ▲ Add salt and the spaghetti to the boiling water, and cook until it is *al dente*.

3 ▲ While the pasta is cooking, warm a large serving bowl and break the eggs into it. Beat in the Parmesan cheese with a fork, and season with salt and pepper.

4 ▲ As soon as the pasta is done, drain it quickly, and mix it into the egg mixture. Pour on the hot bacon and its fat. Stir well. The heat from the pasta and bacon fat will cook the eggs. Serve immediately.

Short Pasta with Cauliflower

Pennoni rigati con cavolfiore

This is a pasta version of cauliflower cheese. The cauliflower water is used to boil the pasta.

Ingredients
1 medium cauliflower
500 ml/16 fl oz/2 cups milk
1 bay leaf
50 g/2 oz/¼ cup butter
50 g/2 oz/½ cup flour
salt and freshly ground black pepper
75 g/3 oz/¾ cup freshly grated Parmesan or Cheddar cheese
500 g/1¼ lb pennoni rigati or other short pasta
serves 6

1 Bring a large pan of water to the boil. Wash the cauliflower well, and separate it into florets. Boil the florets until they are just tender, about 8–10 minutes. Remove them from the pan with a strainer or slotted spoon. Chop the cauliflower into bite-size pieces and set aside. Do not discard the cooking water.

2 ▲ Make a béchamel sauce by gently heating the milk with the bay leaf in a small saucepan. Do not let it boil. Melt the butter in a medium heavy saucepan. Add the flour, and mix it in well with a wire whisk ensuring there are no lumps. Cook for 2–3 minutes, but do not let the butter burn.

3 Strain the hot milk into the flour and butter mixture all at once, and mix smoothly with the whisk.

4 Bring the sauce to the boil, stirring constantly, and cook for 4–5 minutes more. Season with salt and pepper. Add the cheese, and stir over low heat until it melts. Stir in the cauliflower.

5 ▲ Bring the cooking water back to the boil. Add salt, and stir in the pasta. Cook until it is *al dente*. Drain, and tip the pasta into a warm serving bowl. Pour over the sauce. Mix well, and serve at once.

Spaghetti with Bacon and Onion

Spaghetti all'amatriciana

This easy sauce is quickly made from ingredients that are almost always at hand.

Ingredients
30 ml/2 tbsp olive oil or lard
115 g/4 oz/½ cup unsmoked streaky bacon, cut into matchsticks
1 small onion, finely chopped
100 ml/4 fl oz/½ cup dry white wine
450 g/1 lb tomatoes, fresh or canned, chopped
¼ tsp thyme leaves
salt and freshly ground black pepper
600 g/1 lb 5 oz spaghetti
freshly grated Parmesan cheese, to serve
serves 6

1 In a medium frying pan, heat the oil or lard. Add the bacon and onion, and cook over low to moderate heat until the onion is golden and the bacon has rendered its fat and is beginning to brown, about 8–10 minutes. Bring a large pan of water to the boil.

2 ▲ Add the wine to the bacon and onion, raise the heat, and cook rapidly until the liquid boils off. Add the tomatoes, thyme, salt and pepper. Cover, and cook over moderate heat for 10–15 minutes.

3 ▲ Meanwhile, add salt to the boiling water, and cook the pasta until it is *al dente*. Drain, toss with the sauce, and serve with the grated Parmesan.

Spaghetti with Olives and Capers

Spaghetti alla puttanesca

This spicy sauce originated in the Naples area, where it was named for the local women of easy virtue. It can be quickly assembled using a few store cupboard ingredients.

Ingredients
60 ml/4 tbsp olive oil
2 cloves garlic, finely chopped
small piece of dried chilli, crumbled
50 g/2 oz can of anchovy fillets, chopped
350 g/12 oz tomatoes, fresh or canned, chopped
115 g/4 oz/⅔ cup stoned black olives
30 g/2 tbsp capers, rinsed
15 ml/1 tbsp tomato purée
400 g/14 oz spaghetti
2 tbsp chopped fresh parsley, to serve
serves 4

1 ▲ Bring a large pan of water to the boil. Heat the oil in a large frying pan. Add the garlic and the dried chilli, and cook for 2–3 minutes until the garlic is just golden.

2 ▲ Add the anchovies, and mash them into the garlic with a fork.

3 ▲ Add the tomatoes, olives, capers and tomato purée. Stir well and cook over moderate heat.

4 Add salt to the boiling water, and put in the spaghetti. Stir, and cook until the pasta is *al dente*. Drain.

5 ▲ Turn the spaghetti into the the sauce. Raise the heat, and cook for 3–4 minutes, turning the pasta constantly. Sprinkle with parsley if desired and serve. Traditionally, no cheese is served with this sauce.

Linguine with Clam and Tomato Sauce *Linguine con vongole*

There are two types of traditional Italian clam sauce for pasta: one with and one without tomatoes. This tomato version can be made with bottled clams if fresh are not available.

Ingredients
1 kg/2 lb fresh clams in their shells, or 350 g/12 oz bottled clams, with their liquid
90 ml/6 tbsp olive oil
1 clove garlic, crushed
400 g/14 oz tomatoes, fresh or canned, very finely chopped
350 g/12 oz linguine
60 ml/4 tbsp chopped fresh parsley
salt and freshly ground black pepper
serves 4

1 ▲ Scrub and rinse the clams well under cold running water. Place them in a large saucepan with a cupful of water, and heat until the clams begin to open. Lift each clam out as soon as it opens, and scoop it out of its shell using a small spoon. Place in a bowl.

2 If the clams are large, chop them into 2 or 3 pieces. Reserve any liquids from the shells in a separate bowl. When all the clams have opened (discard any that do not open) pour the cooking liquids into the juices from the clams, and strain them through a piece of paper towel to remove any sand. If using bottled clams, use the liquid from the jar.

3 Bring a large pan of water to the boil for the pasta. Place the olive oil in a medium saucepan with the garlic. Cook over moderate heat until the garlic is golden.

4 ▲ Remove the garlic and discard. Add the chopped tomatoes to the oil, and pour in the clam liquid. Mix well and cook over low to moderate heat until the sauce begins to dry out and thicken slightly. Add salt and the pasta to the boiling water.

5 ▲ A minute or two before the pasta is ready to be drained, stir the parsley and the clams into the tomato sauce, and raise the heat. Add some freshly ground black pepper, and taste for seasoning. Drain the pasta, and turn it into a serving bowl. Pour on the hot sauce, and mix well before serving.

9/10

Spaghetti with Mussels

Spaghetti con cozze

Mussels are popular in all the coastal regions of Italy, and are delicious with pasta. This simple dish is greatly improved by using the freshest mussels available.

Ingredients

1 kg/2 lb fresh mussels, in their shells
75 ml/5 tbsp olive oil
3 cloves garlic, finely chopped
60 ml/4 tbsp chopped fresh parsley
60 ml/4 tbsp white wine
400 g/14 oz spaghetti
salt and freshly ground black pepper
serves 4

1 ▲ Scrub the mussels well under cold running water, cutting off the "beard" with a small sharp knife.

2 ▲ Bring a large pan of water to the boil for the pasta. Place the mussels with a cupful of water in another large saucepan over moderate heat. As soon as they open, lift them out one by one.

3 ▲ When all the mussels have opened (discard any that do not), strain the liquid in the saucepan through a layer of paper towels and reserve until needed.

4 ▲ Heat the oil in a large frying pan. Add the garlic and parsley, and cook for 2–3 minutes. Add the mussels, their strained juices and the wine. Cook over moderate heat. Meanwhile add salt to the boiling water, and drop in the pasta.

5 ▲ Add a generous amount of freshly ground black pepper to the sauce. Taste for seasoning, adding salt as necessary.

6 ▲ Drain the pasta when it is *al dente*. Tip it into the frying pan with the sauce, and stir well over moderate heat for 3–4 minutes more. Serve at once, without cheese.

~ COOK'S TIP ~

Mussels should be firmly closed when fresh. If a mussel is slightly open, pinch it closed. If it remains closed on its own, it is alive. If it remains open, discard it. Fresh mussels should be consumed as soon as possible after being purchased. They may be kept in a bowl of cold water in the refrigerator.

Pasta with Fresh Sardine Sauce

Pasta con sarde

In this classic Sicilian dish, fresh sardines are combined with raisins and pine nuts.

Ingredients
30 g/1 ¼ oz/3 tbsp sultanas
450 g/1 lb fresh sardines
90 ml/6 tbsp breadcrumbs
1 small fennel bulb
90 ml/6 tbsp olive oil
1 medium onion, very thinly sliced
30 g/1 ¼ oz/3 tbsp pine nuts
½ tsp fennel seeds
salt and freshly ground black pepper
400 g/14 oz long hollow pasta such as percatelli, zite, or bucatini
serves 4

1 Soak the sultanas in warm water for 15 minutes. Drain and pat dry.

2 ▲ Clean the sardines. Open each one out flat and remove the central bones and head. Wash well and shake dry. Sprinkle with breadcrumbs.

3 ▲ Coarsely chop the top fronds of fennel and reserve. Pull off a few outer leaves and wash. Fill a large pan with enough water to cook the pasta. Add the fennel leaves and bring to the boil.

4 ▲ Heat the oil in a large frying pan and sauté the onion lightly until soft. Remove to a side dish. Add the sardines, a few at a time, and cook over moderate heat until golden on both sides, turning them once carefully. When all the sardines have been cooked, gently return them to the pan. Add the onion, and the sultanas, pine nuts and fennel seeds. Season with salt and pepper.

5 ▲ Take about 60 ml/4 tbsp of the boiling water for the pasta, and add it to the sauce. Add salt to the boiling water, and drop in the pasta. Cook until it is *al dente*. Drain, and remove the fennel leaves. Dress the pasta with the sauce. Divide between individual serving plates, arranging several sardines on each. Sprinkle with the reserved chopped fennel tops before serving.

Baked Macaroni with Cheese

Maccheroni gratinati al forno

This delicious dish is perhaps less common in Italy than other pasta dishes, but has become a family favourite around the world.

Ingredients
500 ml/16 fl oz/2 cups milk
1 bay leaf
3 blades mace, or pinch of grated nutmeg
50 g/2 oz/4 tbsp butter
35 g/1½ oz/⅓ cup flour
salt and freshly ground black pepper
175 g/6 oz/1½ cups grated Parmesan or Cheddar cheese, or a combination of both
40 g/1¾ oz/⅓ cup breadcrumbs
450 g/1 lb macaroni or other short hollow pasta
serves 6

1 Make a béchamel sauce by gently heating the milk with the bay leaf and mace in a small saucepan. Do not let it boil. Melt the butter in a medium heavy saucepan. Add the flour, and mix it in well with a wire whisk. Cook for 2–3 minutes, but do not let the butter burn. Strain the hot milk into the flour and butter mixture all at once, and mix smoothly with the whisk. Bring the sauce to the boil, stirring constantly, and cook for 4–5 minutes more.

2 ▲ Season with salt and pepper, and the nutmeg if no mace has been used. Add all but 30 ml/2 tbsp of the cheese, and stir over low heat until it melts. Place a layer of plastic film right on the surface of the sauce to stop a skin from forming, and set aside.

3 ▲ Bring a large pan of water to the boil. Preheat the oven to 200°C/400°F/ gas 6. Grease an ovenproof dish, and sprinkle with some breadcrumbs. Add salt and the pasta to the boiling water, and cook until it is barely *al dente*. Do not overcook, as the pasta will get a second cooking in the oven.

4 ▲ Drain the pasta, and combine it with the sauce. Pour it into the prepared ovenproof dish. Sprinkle the top with the remaining breadcrumbs and grated cheese, and place in the centre of the preheated oven. Bake for 20 minutes.

Penne with Tuna and Mozzarella *Penne con tonno e mozzarella*

This tasty sauce is quickly made from store-cupboard ingredients, with the addition of fresh mozzarella. If possible, use tuna canned in olive oil.

Ingredients
400 g/14 oz penne, or other short pasta
15 ml/1 tbsp capers, in brine or salt
2 cloves garlic
45 g/3 tbsp chopped fresh parsley
1 × 200 g/7 oz can of tuna, drained
75 ml/5 tbsp olive oil
salt and freshly ground black pepper
115 g/4 oz/⅔ cup mozzarella cheese, cut into small dice
serves 4

1 Bring a large pan of salted water to the boil and drop in the pasta.

2 ▲ Rinse the capers well in water. Chop them finely with the garlic. Combine with the parsley and the tuna. Stir in the oil, and season with salt and pepper, if necessary.

3 ▲ Drain the pasta when it is just *al dente*. Tip it into a large frying pan. Add the tuna sauce and the diced mozzarella, and cook over moderate heat, stirring constantly, until the cheese just begins to melt. Serve at once.

Spaghettini with Vodka and Caviar *Spaghettini con vodka e caviale*

This is an elegant yet easy way to serve spaghettini. In Rome it is an after-theatre favourite.

Ingredients
60 ml/4 tbsp olive oil
3 spring onions, thinly sliced
1 clove garlic, finely chopped
100 ml/4 fl oz/½ cup vodka
150 ml/¼ pint/⅔ cup double cream
75 g/3 oz/½ cup black or red caviar
salt and freshly ground black pepper
400 g/14 oz spaghettini
serves 4

1 ▲ Heat the oil in a small frying pan. Add the spring onions and garlic, and cook gently for 4–5 minutes.

2 ▲ Add the vodka and cream, and cook over low heat for about 5–8 minutes more.

~ COOK'S TIP ~

The finest caviar is salted sturgeon roe. Red "caviar" is dog salmon roe, cheaper and often saltier than sturgeon roe, as is the black-dyed lump-fish roe.

3 ▲ Remove from the heat and stir in the caviar. Season with salt and pepper as necessary.

4 Meanwhile, cook the spaghettini in a large pan of rapidly boiling salted water until *al dente*. Drain the pasta, and toss immediately with the sauce.

Pasta Bows with Prawns and Peas *Farfalle con gamberetti e piselli*

A small amount of saffron in the sauce gives this dish a lovely golden colour.

Ingredients
45 ml/3 tbsp olive oil
25 g/1 oz/2 tbsp butter
2 spring onions, chopped
350 g/12 oz fresh or frozen peeled prawns
225 g/8 oz/1 1/4 cups frozen petit pois or peas, thawed
400 g/14 oz farfalle
250 ml/8 fl oz/1 cup dry white wine
a few strands fresh saffron or 1/8 tsp powdered saffron
salt and freshly ground black pepper
30 ml/2 tbsp chopped fresh fennel or dill, to serve
serves 4

1 Bring a large pan of water to the boil. Heat the oil and butter in a large frying pan and sauté the spring onions lightly. Add the prawns and peas, and cook for 2–3 minutes.

2 ▲ Add salt and the pasta to the boiling water. Stir the wine and saffron into the prawn mixture. Raise the heat and cook until the wine is reduced by about half. Add salt and pepper to taste. Cover the pan and reduce the heat to low.

3 ▲ Drain the pasta when it is *al dente*. Add it to the pan with the sauce. Stir over high heat for 2–3 minutes, coating the pasta with the sauce. Sprinkle with the fresh herbs, and serve at once.

Short Pasta with Spring Vegetables *Pasta primavera*

This colourful sauce makes the most of new crops of fresh tender spring vegetables.

Ingredients
1 or 2 small young carrots
2 spring onions
150 g/6 oz/1 cup courgettes
2 tomatoes
75 g/3 oz/1/2 cup shelled peas, fresh or frozen
75 g/3 oz/1/2 cup green beans
1 yellow pepper
60 ml/4 tbsp olive oil
25 g/1 oz/2 tbsp butter
1 clove garlic, finely chopped
5–6 leaves fresh basil, torn into pieces
salt and freshly ground black pepper
500 g/1 1/4 lb/5 cups short coloured or plain pasta such as fusilli, penne or farfalle
freshly grated Parmesan cheese, to serve
serves 6

1 Cut all the vegetables into small, bite-size pieces.

2 ▲ Heat the oil and butter in a large frying pan. Add the chopped vegetables, and cook over moderate heat for 5–6 minutes, stirring occasionally. Add the garlic and the basil, and season with salt and pepper. Cover the pan, and cook for 5–8 minutes more, or until the vegetables are just tender.

3 ▲ Meanwhile, cook the pasta in a large pan of rapidly boiling salted water until *al dente*. Before draining it, reserve a cupful of the pasta water.

4 Turn the pasta into the pan with the sauce, and mix well to distribute the vegetables. If the sauce seems too dry, add a few tablespoons of the reserved pasta water. Serve with the Parmesan passed separately.

Baked Seafood Spaghetti

Spaghetti al cartoccio

In this dish, each portion is baked and served in an individual packet which is then opened at the table. Use oven parchment or aluminium foil to make the packets.

Ingredients

450 g/1 lb fresh mussels
100 ml/4 fl oz/½ cup dry white wine
60 ml/4 tbsp olive oil
2 cloves garlic, finely chopped
450 g/1 lb tomatoes, fresh or canned, peeled and finely chopped
400 g/14 oz spaghetti or other long pasta
225 g/8 oz peeled and deveined prawns, fresh or frozen
30 ml/2 tbsp chopped fresh parsley
salt and freshly ground black pepper
serves 4

1 ▲ Scrub the mussels well under cold running water, cutting off the "beard" with a small sharp knife. Place the mussels and the wine in a large saucepan and heat until they open.

2 ▲ Lift out the mussels and remove to a side dish. (Discard any that do not open.) Strain the cooking liquid through paper towels, and reserve until needed. Preheat the oven to 150°C/300°F/gas 2.

3 ▲ Bring a large pan of water to the boil. In a medium saucepan, heat the oil and garlic together for 1–2 minutes. Add the tomatoes, and cook over moderate to high heat until they soften. Stir in 150 ml/6 fl oz/¾ cup of the cooking liquid from the mussels. Add salt and the pasta to the boiling water, and cook until it is just *al dente*.

4 ▲ Just before draining the pasta, add the prawns and parsley to the tomato sauce. Cook for 2 minutes. Taste for seasoning, adding salt and pepper as desired. Remove from the heat.

~ VARIATION ~

Bottled mussels or clams may be substituted for fresh shellfish in this recipe. Add them to the tomato sauce with the prawns.

5 ▲ Prepare 4 pieces of parchment paper or foil approximately 30 cm × 45 cm (12 in × 18 in). Place each sheet in the centre of a shallow bowl. Turn the drained pasta into a mixing bowl. Add the tomato sauce and mix well. Stir in the mussels.

6 ▲ Divide the pasta and seafood between the four pieces of paper, placing a mound in the centre of each, and twisting the paper ends together to make a closed packet. (The bowl under the paper will stop the sauce from spilling while the paper parcels are being closed.) Arrange on a large baking tray, and place in the centre of the preheated oven. Bake for 8–10 minutes. Place one unopened packet on each individual serving plate.

Tuna Pasta Salad

Insalata di pasta con tonno

This easy pasta salad uses canned beans and tuna for a quick main dish.

Ingredients

450 g/1 lb short pasta such as ruote, macaroni or farfalle
60 ml/4 tbsp olive oil
2 × 200 g/7 oz cans tuna, drained
2 × 400 g/14 oz cans cannellini or borlotti beans, rinsed and drained
1 small red onion
2 sticks celery
juice of 1 lemon
30 ml/2 tbsp chopped fresh parsley
salt and freshly ground black pepper
serves 6–8

1 Cook the pasta in a large pan of rapidly boiling salted water until it is *al dente*. Drain, and rinse under cold water to stop cooking. Drain well and turn into a large bowl. Toss with the olive oil, and set aside. Allow to cool completely before mixing with the other ingredients.

2 ▲ Mix the flaked tuna and the beans into the cooked pasta. Slice the onion and celery very thinly and add them to the pasta.

3 ▲ Combine the lemon juice with the parsley. Mix into the other ingredients. Season with salt and pepper. Allow the salad to stand for at least 1 hour before serving.

Chicken Pasta Salad

Insalata di pasta con pollo

This salad uses leftover chicken from a roast, or a cold poached chicken breast.

Ingredients

350 g/12 oz short pasta, such as mezze rigatoni, fusilli or penne
45 ml/3 tbsp olive oil
225 g/8 oz/1½ cups cold cooked chicken
2 small red and yellow peppers (about 200 g/7 oz)
50 g/2 oz/⅓ cup stoned green olives
4 spring onions, chopped
45 ml/3 tbsp mayonnaise
1 tsp Worcestershire sauce
15 ml/1 tbsp wine vinegar
salt and freshly ground black pepper
a few leaves fresh basil, to garnish
serves 4

1 Cook the pasta in a large pan of rapidly boiling salted water until it is *al dente*. Drain, and rinse under cold water to stop the cooking. Drain well and turn into a large bowl. Toss with the olive oil, and set aside. Allow to cool completely.

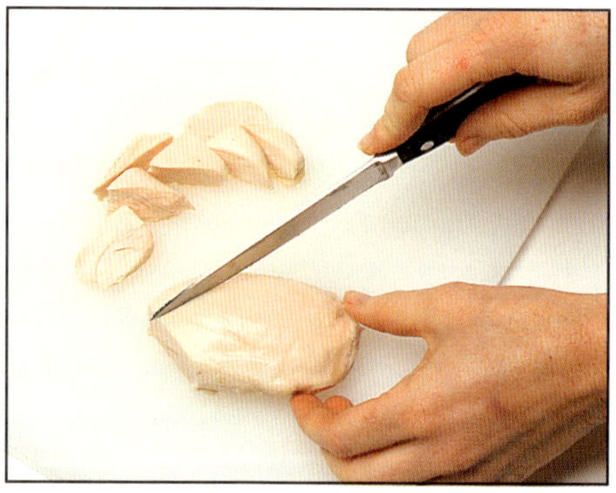

2 ▲ Cut the chicken into bite-size pieces, removing any bones. Cut the peppers into small pieces, removing the seeds and stems.

3 ▲ Combine all the ingredients except the pasta in a medium bowl. Taste for seasoning, then mix into the pasta. Garnish with the basil, and serve chilled.

Wholewheat Pasta Salad

Insalata di pasta integrale

This substantial vegetarian salad is easily assembled from any combination of seasonal vegetables. Use raw or lightly blanched vegetables, or a mixture of both.

Ingredients
450 g/1 lb short wholewheat pasta, such as fusilli or penne
45 ml/3 tbsp olive oil
2 medium carrots
1 small bunch broccoli
175 g/6 oz/1 cup shelled peas, fresh or frozen
1 red or yellow pepper
2 sticks celery
4 spring onions
1 large tomato
75 g/3 oz/½ cup stoned olives
For the dressing
45 ml/3 tbsp wine or balsamic vinegar
60 ml/4 tbsp olive oil
15 ml/1 tbsp Dijon style mustard
15 ml/1 tbsp sesame seeds
10 ml/2 tsp chopped mixed fresh herbs, such as parsley, thyme and basil
salt and freshly ground black pepper
115 g/4 oz/⅔ cup diced Cheddar or mozzarella, or a combination of both
serves 8

1 Cook the pasta in a large pan of rapidly boiling salted water until it is *al dente*. Drain, and rinse under cold water to stop the cooking. Drain well and turn into a large bowl. Toss with 45 ml/3 tbsp of the olive oil, and set aside. Allow to cool completely before mixing with the other ingredients.

2 ▲ Lightly blanch the carrots, broccoli and peas in a large pan of boiling water. Refresh under cold water. Drain well.

3 ▲ Chop the carrots and broccoli into bite-size pieces and add to the pasta with the peas. Slice the pepper, celery, spring onions and tomato into small pieces. Add them to the salad with the olives.

4 ▲ Make the dressing in a small bowl by combining the vinegar with the oil and mustard. Stir in the sesame seeds and herbs. Mix the dressing into the salad. Taste for seasoning, adding salt, pepper or more oil and vinegar as necessary. Stir in the cheese. Allow the salad to stand for 15 minutes before serving.

Pasta Salad with Olives

Insalata di pasta con olive

This delicious salad combines all the flavours of the Mediterranean. It is an excellent way of serving pasta and is particularly nice on hot summer days.

Ingredients
450 g/1 lb short pasta, such as medium shells, farfalle or penne
60 ml/4 tbsp extra-virgin olive oil
10 sun-dried tomatoes, thinly sliced
30 ml/2 tbsp capers, in brine or salted
115 g/4 oz/⅔ cup black olives, stoned
2 cloves garlic, finely chopped
45 ml/3 tbsp balsamic vinegar
salt and freshly ground black pepper
45 ml/3 tbsp chopped fresh parsley
serves 6

1 ▲ Cook the pasta in a large pan of rapidly boiling salted water until it is *al dente*. Drain, and rinse under cold water to stop the cooking. Drain well and turn into a large bowl. Toss with the olive oil, and set aside.

2 ▲ Soak the tomatoes in a bowl of hot water for 10 minutes. Do not discard the water. Rinse the capers well. If they have been preserved in salt, soak them in a little hot water for 10 minutes. Rinse again.

3 ▲ Combine the olives, tomatoes, capers, garlic and vinegar in a small bowl. Season with salt and pepper.

4 ▲ Stir this mixture into the pasta, and toss well. Add 2 or 3 spoons of the tomato soaking water if the salad seems too dry. Toss with the parsley, and allow to stand for 15 minutes before serving.

Fettuccine with Ham and Cream

Fettuccine con prosciutto

Prosciutto is perfect for this rich and delicious dish, which makes an elegant first course.

Ingredients

115 g/4 oz/½ cup prosciutto crudo or other unsmoked ham (raw or cooked)
50 g/2 oz/¼ cup butter
2 shallots, very finely chopped
salt and freshly ground black pepper
150 ml/¼ pint/⅔ cup double cream
350 g/12 oz fettuccine (made with 3 eggs)
50 g/2 oz/½ cup grated Parmesan cheese
sprig fresh parsley, to garnish
serves 4

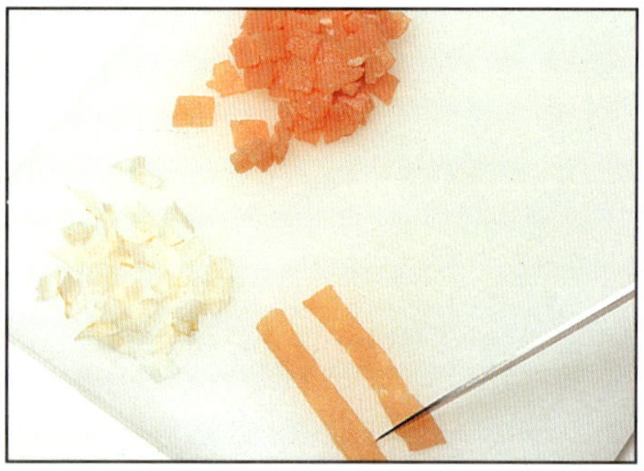

1 ▲ Cut the fat from the ham, and chop both lean and fat parts separately into small squares.

2 ▲ Melt the butter in a medium frying pan, and add the shallots and the squares of ham fat. Cook until golden. Add the lean ham, and cook for 2 minutes more. Season with black pepper. Stir in the cream, and keep warm over low heat while the pasta is cooking.

3 ▲ Boil the pasta in a large pan of rapidly boiling salted water. Drain when *al dente*. Turn into a warmed serving bowl, and toss with the sauce. Stir in the cheese and serve at once, garnished with a sprig of parsley.

~ VARIATION ~

Substitute 170 g/6 oz fresh or frozen peas for the ham. Add to the pan with the shallots.

Tagliatelle with Smoked Salmon

Tagliatelle con salmone

In Italy smoked salmon is imported, and quite expensive. This elegant creamy sauce makes a little go a long way. Use a mixture of green and white pasta if you wish.

Ingredients

175 g/6 oz/¾ cup smoked salmon slices or ends, fresh or frozen
300 ml/½ pint/1¼ cups single cream
pinch of ground mace or nutmeg
350 g/12 oz green and white tagliatelle (made with 3 eggs)
salt and freshly ground black pepper
45 ml/3 tbsp chopped fresh chives, to garnish
serves 4–5

1 Cut the salmon into thin strips about 5 cm/2 in long. Place in a bowl with the cream and the mace or nutmeg. Stir, cover, and allow to stand for at least 2 hours in a cool place.

2 ▲ Bring a large pan of water to the boil for the pasta. While the water is heating, gently warm the cream and salmon mixture in a small saucepan without boiling it.

3 ▲ Add salt to the boiling water. Drop in the pasta all at once. Drain when it is just *al dente*. Pour the sauce over the pasta and mix well. Season and garnish with the chives.

Baked Lasagne with Meat Sauce

Lasagne al forno

This lasagne made from egg pasta with home-made meat and béchamel sauces is exquisite.

Ingredients
1 recipe Bolognese Meat Sauce
egg pasta sheets made with 3 eggs, or 400 g/14 oz dried lasagne
115 g/4 oz/1 cup grated Parmesan cheese
40 g/1½ oz/3 tbsp butter

For the béchamel sauce
700 ml/1¼ pints/3 cups milk
1 bay leaf
3 blades mace
115 g/4 oz/½ cup butter
75 g/3 oz/¾ cup flour
salt and freshly ground black pepper

serves 8–10

1 Prepare the meat sauce and set aside. Butter a large shallow baking dish, preferably rectangular or square.

2 Make the béchamel sauce by gently heating the milk with the bay leaf and mace in a small saucepan. Melt the butter in a medium heavy saucepan. Add the flour, and mix it in well with a wire whisk. Cook for 2–3 minutes. Strain the hot milk into the flour and butter, and mix smoothly with the whisk. Bring the sauce to the boil, stirring constantly, and cook for 4–5 minutes more. Season with salt and pepper, and set aside.

3 ▲ Make the pasta. Do not let it dry out before cutting it into rectangles approximately 11 cm/4½ in wide and the same length as the baking dish (this will make it easier to assemble). Preheat the oven to 200°C/400°F/gas 6.

4 ▲ Bring a very large pan of water to the boil. Place a large bowl of cold water near the stove. Cover a large work surface with a tablecloth. Add salt to the rapidly boiling water. Drop in 3 or 4 of the egg pasta rectangles. Cook very briefly, about 30 seconds. Remove them from the pan using a slotted spoon, and drop them into the bowl of cold water for about 30 seconds. Pull them out of the water, shaking off the excess water. Lay them out flat without overlapping on the tablecloth. Continue with all the remaining pasta and trimmings.

5 ▲ To assemble the lasagne, have all the elements at hand: the baking dish, béchamel and meat sauces, pasta strips, grated Parmesan and butter. Spread one large spoonful of the meat sauce over the bottom of the dish. Arrange a layer of pasta in the dish, cutting it with a sharp knife so that it fits well inside the dish.

6 ▲ Cover with a thin layer of meat sauce, then one of béchamel. Sprinkle with a little cheese. Repeat the layers in the same order, ending with a layer of pasta coated with béchamel. Do not make more than about 6 layers of pasta. (If you have a lot left over, make another small lasagne in a little ovenproof dish.) Use the pasta trimmings to patch any gaps in the pasta. Sprinkle the top with Parmesan, and dot with butter.

7 Bake in the preheated oven for 20 minutes or until brown on top. Remove from the oven and allow to stand for 5 minutes before serving. Serve directly from the baking dish, cutting out rectangular or square sections for each helping.

~ VARIATION ~

If you are using dried or bought pasta, follow step 4, but boil the lasagne in just two batches, and stop the cooking about 4 minutes before the recommended cooking time on the packet has elapsed. Rinse in cold water and lay the pasta out the same way as for the egg pasta.

Tagliolini with Asparagus

Tagliolini con asparagi

Tagliolini are very thin home-made egg noodles, more delicate in texture than spaghetti. They go well with this subtle cream sauce flavoured with asparagus.

Ingredients
450 g/1 lb fresh asparagus
egg pasta sheets made with 2 eggs, or 350 g/12 oz fresh tagliolini or other egg noodles
50 g/2 oz/¼ cup butter
3 spring onions, finely chopped
3–4 leaves fresh mint or basil, finely chopped
150 ml/¼ pint/⅔ cup double cream
salt and freshly ground black pepper
50 g/2 oz/½ cup freshly grated Parmesan cheese
serves 4

1 ▲ Peel the asparagus by inserting a small sharp knife at the base of the stalks and pulling upwards towards the tips, drop them into a large pan of rapidly boiling water, and boil until just tender, 4–6 minutes.

2 ▲ Remove from the water, reserving the cooking water. Cut the tips off, and then cut the stalks into 4 cm/1½ in pieces. Set aside.

3 Make the egg pasta sheets, and fold and cut into thin noodles, or feed them through the narrowest cutters of a machine. Open the noodles out, and let them dry for at least 5–10 minutes.

4 ▲ Melt the butter in a large frying pan. Add the spring onions and herbs, and cook for 3–4 minutes. Stir in the cream and asparagus, and heat gently, but do not boil. Season to taste.

5 Bring the asparagus cooking water back to the boil. Add salt. Drop the noodles in all at once. Cook until just tender (freshly made noodles will cook in 30–60 seconds). Drain

6 ▲ Turn the pasta into the pan with the sauce, raise heat slightly, and mix well. Stir in the Parmesan. Mix well and serve at once.

Ravioli with Ricotta and Spinach

Ravioli ripieni di magro

Home-made ravioli are fun to make, and can be stuffed with different meat, cheese or vegetable fillings. This filling is easy to make, and lighter than the normal meat variety.

Ingredients
400 g/14 oz fresh spinach or 175 g/6 oz frozen spinach
175 g/6 oz/¾ cup ricotta cheese
1 egg
50 g/2 oz/½ cup grated Parmesan cheese
pinch of grated nutmeg
salt and freshly ground black pepper
egg pasta sheets made with 3 eggs

For the sauce
75 g/3 oz/⅓ cup butter
5–6 sprigs fresh sage

serves 4

1 Wash fresh spinach well in several changes of water. Place in a saucepan with only the water that is clinging to the leaves. Cover, and cook until tender, about 5 minutes. Drain. Cook frozen spinach according to the instructions on the package. When the spinach is cool, squeeze out as much moisture as possible. Chop finely.

2 Combine the chopped spinach with the ricotta, egg, Parmesan and nutmeg. Mix well. Season with salt and pepper. Cover the bowl and set aside.

3 Prepare the sheets of egg pasta. Roll out very thinly by hand or machine. Do not let the pasta dry out.

4 ▲ Place small teaspoons of filling along the pasta in rows 5 cm/2 in apart. Cover with another sheet of pasta, pressing down gently to avoid forming air pockets.

5 ▲ Use a fluted pastry wheel to cut between the rows to form small squares with filling in the centre of each. If the edges do not stick well, moisten with milk or water, and press together with a fork. Place the ravioli on a lightly floured surface, and allow to dry for at least 30 minutes. Turn occasionally so they dry on both sides. Bring a large pan of salted water to the boil.

6 Heat the butter and sage together over very low heat, taking care that the butter melts but does not darken.

7 ▲ Drop the ravioli into the boiling water. Stir gently to prevent them from sticking. They will be cooked in very little time, about 4–5 minutes. Drain carefully and arrange in individual serving dishes. Spoon on the sauce, and serve at once.

Baked Vegetable Lasagne

Lasagne al forno con funghi e pomodori

Following the principles of the classic meat sauce lasagne, other combinations of ingredients can be used most effectively. This vegetarian lasagne uses fresh vegetables and herbs.

Ingredients

egg pasta sheets made with 3 eggs
30 ml/2 tbsp olive oil
1 medium onion, very finely chopped
500 g/1¼ lb tomatoes, fresh or canned, chopped
salt and freshly ground black pepper
675 g/1½ lb cultivated or wild mushrooms, or a combination of both
75 g/3 oz/⅓ cup butter
2 cloves garlic, finely chopped
juice of ½ lemon
1 litre/1¾ pints/4½ cups béchamel sauce
175 g/6 oz/1½ cups freshly grated Parmesan or Cheddar cheese, or a combination of both

serves 8

1 Butter a large shallow baking dish, preferably rectangular or square.

2 ▲ Make the egg pasta. Do not let it dry out before cutting it into rectangles approximately 11 cm/4½ in wide and the same length as the baking dish (this will make it easier to assemble).

3 In a small frying pan heat the oil and sauté the onion until translucent. Add the chopped tomatoes, and cook for 6–8 minutes, stirring often. Season with salt and pepper, and set aside.

4 ▲ Wipe the mushrooms carefully with a damp cloth. Slice finely. Heat 35 g/1½ oz of the butter in a frying pan, and when it is bubbling, add the mushrooms. Cook until the mushrooms start to exude their juices. Add the garlic and lemon juice, and season with salt and pepper. Cook until the liquids have almost all evaporated and the mushrooms are starting to brown. Set aside.

5 ▲ Preheat the oven to 200°C/400°F/gas 6. Bring a very large pan of water to the boil. Place a large bowl of cold water near the stove. Cover a large work surface with a tablecloth. Add salt to the rapidly boiling water. Drop in 3 or 4 of the egg pasta rectangles. Cook very briefly, about 30 seconds. Remove them from the pan using a slotted spoon, and drop them into the bowl of cold water for about 30 seconds. Remove and lay out to dry. Continue with the remaining pasta.

6 ▲ To assemble the lasagne have all the elements at hand: the baking dish, fillings, pasta, cheeses and butter. Spread one large spoonful of the béchamel sauce over the bottom of the dish. Arrange a layer of pasta in the dish, cutting it with a sharp knife so that it fits well. Cover the pasta with a thin layer of mushrooms, then one of béchamel sauce. Sprinkle with a little cheese.

7 ▲ Make another layer of pasta, spread with a thin layer of tomatoes, and then one of béchamel. Sprinkle with cheese. Repeat the layers in the same order, ending with a layer of pasta coated with béchamel. Do not make more than about 6 layers of pasta. Use the pasta trimmings to patch any gaps in the pasta. Sprinkle with cheese, and dot with butter.

8 Bake for 20 minutes. Remove from the oven and allow to stand for 5 minutes before serving.

Tortelli with Pumpkin Stuffing

Tortelli di zucca

During autumn and winter the northern Italian markets are full of bright orange pumpkins, which are used to make soups and pasta dishes. This dish is a speciality of Mantua.

Ingredients

1 kg/2 lb pumpkin (weight with shell)
75 g/3 oz/1½ cups amaretti biscuits, crushed
2 eggs
75 g/3 oz/¾ cup freshly grated Parmesan cheese
pinch of grated nutmeg
salt and freshly ground black pepper
plain breadcrumbs, as required
egg pasta sheets made with 3 eggs

To serve

115 g/4 oz/½ cup butter
75 g/3 oz/¾ cup freshly grated Parmesan cheese

serves 6–8

1 Preheat the oven to 190°C/375°/gas 5. Cut the pumpkin into 10 cm/4 in pieces. Leave the skin on. Place the pumpkin pieces in a covered casserole, and bake for 45–50 minutes. When cool, cut off the skins. Purée the flesh in a food mill or food processor or press through a sieve.

2 ▲ Combine the pumpkin purée with the biscuit crumbs, eggs, Parmesan and nutmeg. Season with salt and pepper. If the mixture is too wet, add 15–30 g/1–2 tbsp of breadcrumbs. Set aside.

3 Prepare the sheets of egg pasta. Roll out very thinly by hand or machine. Do not let the pasta dry out before filling it.

4 ▲ Place tablespoons of filling every 6–7 cm/2½ in along the pasta in rows 5 cm/2 in apart. Cover with another sheet of pasta, and press down gently. Use a fluted pastry wheel to cut between the rows to form rectangles with filling in the centre of each. Place the tortelli on a lightly floured surface, and allow to dry for at least 30 minutes. Turn them occasionally so they dry on both sides.

5 Bring a large pan of salted water to the boil. Gently heat the butter over very low heat, taking care that it does not darken.

6 ▲ Drop the tortelli into the boiling water. Stir to prevent from sticking. They will be cooked in 4–5 minutes. Drain and arrange in individual dishes. Spoon on the melted butter, sprinkle with Parmesan, and serve.

Stuffed Pasta Half-moons

Mezzelune ripiene di formaggi

These stuffed egg pasta half-moons are filled with a delicate mixture of cheeses. They make an elegant first course.

Ingredients
225 g/8 oz/1¼ cups fresh ricotta or curd cheese
225 g/8 oz/1¼ cups mozzarella cheese
115 g/4 oz/1 cup freshly grated Parmesan cheese
2 eggs
45 ml/3 tbsp finely chopped fresh basil
salt and freshly ground black pepper
egg pasta sheets made with 3 eggs
milk

For the sauce
450 g/1 lb fresh tomatoes
30 ml/2 tbsp olive oil
1 small onion, very finely chopped
90 ml/6 tbsp cream

serves 6–8

1 ▲ Press the ricotta or curd cheese through a sieve or strainer. Chop the mozzarella into very small cubes. Combine all three cheeses in a bowl. Beat in the eggs and basil, season and set aside.

2 Make the sauce by dropping the tomatoes into a small pan of boiling water for 1 minute. Remove, and peel using a small sharp knife to pull the skins off. Chop the tomatoes finely. Heat the oil in a medium saucepan. Add the onion and cook over moderate heat until soft and translucent. Add the tomatoes and cook until soft, about 15 minutes. Season with salt and pepper. (The sauce may be pressed through a sieve to make it smooth.) Set aside.

3 Prepare the sheets of egg pasta. Roll out very thinly by hand or machine. Do not let the pasta dry out.

4 ▲ Using a glass or pastry cutter, cut out rounds approximately 10 cm/4 in in diameter. Spoon one large tablespoon of the filling onto one half of each pasta round and fold over.

5 Press the edges closed with a fork. Re-roll any trimmings and use to make more rounds. Allow the half-moons to dry for at least 10–15 minutes. Turn them over so they dry evenly.

6 Bring a large pan of salted water to the boil. Place the tomato sauce in a small saucepan and heat gently while the pasta is cooking. Stir in the cream. Do not boil.

7 Gently drop in the stuffed pasta, and stir carefully to prevent them from sticking. Cook for 5–7 minutes. Scoop them out of the water, drain carefully, and arrange in individual dishes. Spoon on some of the sauce, and serve at once.

Cannelloni Stuffed with Meat

Cannelloni ripieni di carne

Cannelloni are rectangles of home-made egg pasta which are spread with a filling, rolled up and baked in a sauce. In this recipe, they are baked in a béchamel sauce.

Ingredients
30 ml/2 tbsp olive oil
1 medium onion, very finely chopped
225 g/8 oz/1½ cups very lean minced beef
75 g/3 oz/½ cup cooked ham, finely chopped
15 ml/1 tbsp chopped fresh parsley
30 ml/2 tbsp tomato purée, softened in 15 ml/1 tbsp warm water
1 egg
salt and freshly ground black pepper
egg pasta sheets made with 2 eggs
750 ml/1¼ pints/3⅔ cups béchamel sauce
50 g/2 oz/½ cup freshly grated Parmesan cheese
40 g/1½ oz/3 tbsp butter
serves 6–8

1 ▲ Prepare the meat filling by heating the oil in a medium saucepan. Add the onion, and sauté gently until translucent. Stir in the beef, crumbling it with a fork, and stirring constantly until it has lost its raw red colour. Cook for 3–4 minutes.

2 ▲ Remove from the heat, and turn the beef mixture into a bowl with the ham and parsley. Add the tomato purée and the egg, and mix well. Season with salt and pepper. Set aside.

3 ▲ Make the egg pasta sheets. Do not let the pasta dry before cutting it into rectangles 12–13 cm/5–6 in long and as wide as they come from the machine (8–9 cm/3 in if you are not using a machine).

4 Bring a very large pan of water to the boil. Place a large bowl of cold water near the stove. Cover a large work surface with a tablecloth. Add salt to the rapidly boiling water. Drop in 3 or 4 of the egg pasta rectangles. Cook very briefly, about 30 seconds. Remove and drop them into the bowl of cold water for about 30 seconds more. Pull them out of the water, shaking off the excess water. Lay them out flat on the tablecloth. Continue with the remaining pasta.

5 Preheat the oven to 220°C/425°F/gas 7. Select a shallow baking dish large enough to accommodate all the cannelloni in one layer. Butter the dish, and smear 30–45 ml/2–3 tbsp of béchamel sauce over the bottom.

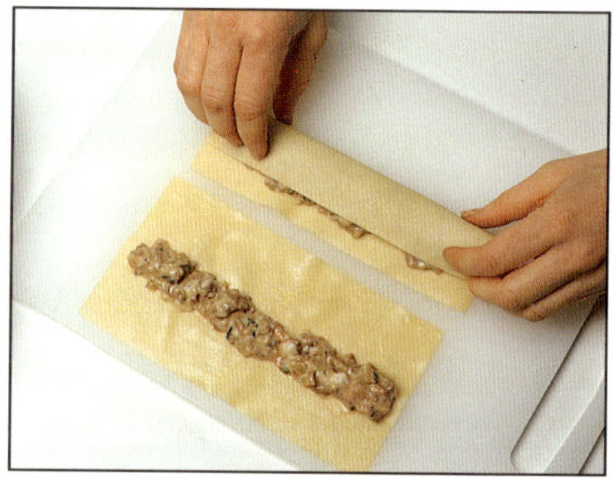

6 ▲ Stir about one third of the sauce into the meat filling. Spread a thin layer of filling on each pasta rectangle. Roll the rectangles up loosely starting from the long side, Swiss-roll style. Place the cannelloni into the baking dish with their open edges down.

7 ▲ Spoon the rest of the sauce over the cannelloni, pushing a little down between each pasta roll. Sprinkle the top with the grated Parmesan, and dot with butter. Bake for about 20 minutes. Allow to rest for 5–8 minutes before serving.

9½/10

Pasta and Dried Bean Soup

Pasta e fagioli

This peasant soup is very thick. In Italy it is made with dried or fresh beans, never canned, and served hot or at room temperature.

Ingredients

300 g/11 oz/1½ cups dried borlotti or cannellini beans (2 BAKED BEAN)

1 × 400 g/14 oz can plum tomatoes, chopped, with their juice

3 cloves garlic, crushed

2 bay leaves

pinch of coarsely ground black pepper

90 ml/6 tbsp olive oil, plus extra to serve (optional)

750 ml/1¼ pint/3½ cups water

10 ml/2 tsp salt

200 g/7 oz/2¼ cups ditalini or other small pasta

45 ml/3 tbsp chopped fresh parsley

freshly grated Parmesan cheese, to serve

serves 4–6

1 Soak the beans in water overnight. Rinse and drain well.

2 Place the beans in a large saucepan and cover with water. Bring to the boil and cook for 10 minutes. Rinse and drain again.

3 ▲ Return the beans to the pan. Add enough water to cover them by 2.5 cm/1 in. Stir in the coarsely chopped tomatoes with their juice, the garlic, bay leaves, black pepper and the oil. Simmer for 1½–2 hours, or until the beans are tender. If necessary, add more water.

4 ▲ Remove the bay leaves. Pass about half of the bean mixture through a food mill, or purée in a food processor. Stir into the pan with the remaining bean mixture. Add the water, and bring the soup to the boil.

5 ▲ Add the salt and the pasta. Stir, and cook until the pasta is just done. Stir in the parsley. Allow to stand for at least 10 minutes before serving. Serve with grated Parmesan passed separately. In Italy a little olive oil is poured into each serving.

Pasta and Lentil Soup

Pasta e lenticchie

The small brown lentils which are grown in central Italy are usually used in this wholesome soup, but green lentils may be substituted if preferred.

Ingredients

225 g/8 oz/1 cup dried green or brown lentils
90 ml/6 tbsp olive oil
50 g/2 oz/¼ cup ham or salt pork, cut into small dice
1 medium onion, finely chopped
1 stick celery, finely chopped
1 carrot, finely chopped
2 litres/3½ pints/9 cups chicken broth or water, or a combination of both
1 leaf fresh sage or ⅛ tsp dried sage
1 sprig fresh thyme or ¼ tsp dried thyme
salt and freshly ground black pepper
175 g/6 oz/2½ cups ditalini or other small soup pasta

serves 4–6

1 ▲ Carefully check the lentils for small stones. Place them in a bowl, covered with cold water, and soak for 2–3 hours. Rinse and drain well.

2 ▲ In a large saucepan, heat the oil and sauté the ham or salt pork for 2–3 minutes. Add the onion, and cook gently until it softens.

3 ▲ Stir in the celery and carrot, and cook for 5 minutes more, stirring frequently. Add the lentils, and stir to coat them in the fats.

4 ▲ Pour in the broth or water and the herbs, and bring the soup to the boil. Cook over moderate heat for about 1 hour or until the lentils are tender. Add salt and pepper to taste.

5 Stir in the pasta, and cook it until it is just done. Allow the soup to stand for a few minutes before serving.

Pasta and Chickpea Soup

Pasta e ceci

Another thick soup from central Italy. The addition of a sprig of fresh rosemary provides a typically Mediterranean flavour.

Ingredients

200 g/7 oz/1 cup dried chickpeas
3 cloves garlic, peeled
1 bay leaf
90 ml/6 tbsp olive oil
pinch of freshly ground black pepper
50 g/2 oz/¼ cup salt pork, pancetta or bacon, diced
1 sprig fresh rosemary
600 ml/1 pint/2½ cups water
150 g/5 oz ditalini or other short hollow pasta
salt, to taste
freshly grated Parmesan cheese, to serve (optional)

serves 4–6

1 ▲ Soak the chickpeas in water overnight. Rinse well and drain. Place the chickpeas in a large saucepan with water to cover. Boil for 15 minutes. Rinse and drain.

~ COOK'S TIP ~

Allow the soup to stand for about 10 minutes before serving. This will allow the flavour and texture to develop.

2 ▲ Return the chickpeas to the pan. Add water to cover, 1 clove of garlic, the bay leaf, 45 ml/3 tbsp of the oil and the ground pepper.

3 ▲ Simmer until tender, about 2 hours, adding more water as necessary. Remove the bay leaf. Pass about half the chickpeas through a food mill or purée in a food processor with a few tablespoons of the cooking liquid. Return the purée to the pan with the rest of the peas and the remaining cooking water.

4 ▲ Sauté the diced pork gently in the remaining oil with the rosemary and 2 cloves of garlic until just golden. Discard the rosemary and garlic.

5 ▲ Stir the pork with its oils into the chickpea mixture.

6 ▲ Add 600 ml/1 pint/2½ cups of water to the chickpeas, and bring to the boil. Correct the seasoning if necessary. Stir in the pasta, and cook until just *al dente*. Pass the Parmesan separately, if desired.

PIZZAS, PASTRIES AND BREAD

Pizzas are fun to make at home. Personalize them with combinations of your favourite ingredients. Italian flatbreads and bread sticks can be topped with herbs and seeds for tasty accompaniments or starters or unusual snacks.

Basic Pizza Dough

Pizza dough is leavened with yeast. It usually rises once before being rolled out and filled. The dough can be baked in pizza pans or baked directly on a flat baking sheet.

Ingredients

25 g/1 oz/2½ tbsp fresh cake yeast or
15 g/½ oz/1½ tbsp active dried yeast
250 ml/8 fl oz/1 cup lukewarm water
pinch of sugar
5 ml/1 tsp salt
350–400 g/12–14 oz/3–3½ cups plain flour, preferably strong

serves 4 as a main course or 8 as an appetizer

1 ▲ Warm a medium mixing bowl by swirling some hot water in it. Drain. Place the yeast in the bowl, and pour on the warm water. Stir in the sugar, mix with a fork, and allow to stand until the yeast has dissolved and starts to foam, 5–10 minutes.

2 ▲ Use a wooden spoon to mix in the salt and about one-third of the flour. Mix in another third of the flour, stirring with the spoon until the dough forms a mass and begins to pull away from the sides of the bowl.

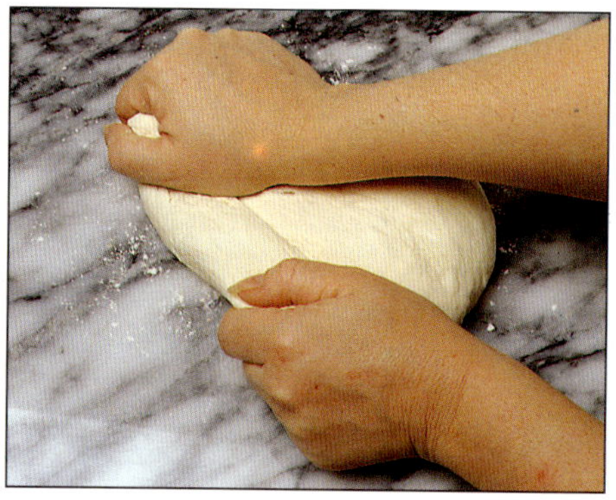

3 ▲ Sprinkle some of the remaining flour onto a smooth work surface. Remove the dough from the bowl and begin to knead it, working in the remaining flour a little at a time. Knead for 8–10 minutes. By the end the dough should be elastic and smooth. Form it into a ball.

4 Lightly oil a mixing bowl. Place the dough in the bowl. Stretch a moistened and wrung-out dish towel across the top of the bowl, and leave it to stand in a warm place until the dough has doubled in volume, about 40–50 minutes or more, depending on the type of yeast used. (If you do not have a warm enough place, turn the oven on to medium heat for 10 minutes before you knead the dough. Turn it off. Place the bowl with the dough in it in the turned-off oven with the door closed and let it rise there.) To test whether the dough has risen enough, poke two fingers into the dough. If the indentations remain, the dough is ready.

5 ▲ Punch the dough down with your fist to release the air. Knead for 1–2 minutes.

6 If you want to make 2 medium pizzas, divide the dough into 2 balls. If you want to make 4 individual pizzas (in pans 26 cm/10½ in in diameter), divide the dough into 4 balls. Pat the ball of dough out into a flat circle on a lightly floured surface. With a rolling pin, roll it out to a thickness of about 5–7 mm/⅜–¼ in. If you are using a pizza pan, roll the dough out about 7 mm/¼ in larger than the size of the pan for the rim of the crust.

7 ▲ Place in the lightly oiled pan, folding the extra dough under to make a thicker rim around the edge. If you are baking the pizza without a round pan, press some of the dough from the centre of the circle towards the edge, to make a thicker rim. Place it on a lightly oiled flat baking sheet. The dough is now ready for filling.

~ COOK'S TIP ~

This basic dough can be used for other recipes in this book, such as Focaccia, Bread sticks, Calzone and Sicilian Closed Pizza. The dough may be frozen at the end of step 7, and thawed before filling.

Wholewheat Pizza Dough

Pizza dough can also be made with wholewheat flour, although it is easier to handle and more elastic if a proportion of white flour is used. This dough can be used in any recipe calling for Basic Pizza Dough.

Ingredients

25 g/1 oz/2½ tbsp fresh cake yeast or 15 g/½ oz/1½ tbsp active dried yeast
250 ml/8 fl oz/1 cup lukewarm water
pinch of sugar
30 ml/2 tbsp olive oil
5 ml/1 tsp salt
150 g/5 oz/1¼ cups plain white flour
250 g/9 oz/2 cups stoneground wholewheat flour

serves 4 as a main course or 8 as an appetizer

1 Warm a medium mixing bowl by swirling some hot water in it. Drain. Place the yeast in the bowl, and pour on the warm water. Stir in the sugar, mix with a fork, and allow to stand until the yeast has dissolved and starts to foam, 5–10 minutes.

2 ▲ Use a wooden spoon to mix in the olive oil and the salt, and the white flour. Mix in about half of the wholewheat flour, stirring with the spoon until the dough forms a mass and begins to pull away from the sides of the bowl.

3 ▲ Proceed with steps 3–7 as for Basic Pizza Dough, punching down the risen dough, and kneading until ready to roll out and place in a pan.

To Make the Dough in a Food Processor

1 ▲ Have all the ingredients ready and measured out. In a small jug or bowl add the yeast to the warm water. Stir in the sugar, and allow to stand until the yeast has dissolved, 5–10 minutes.

2 ▲ Fit the food processor with the metal blades. Place the salt and three-quarters of the flour in the bowl of the food processor. Turn it on, and pour in the yeast mixture and olive oil through the opening at the top. Continue processing until the dough forms one or two balls. Turn the machine off, open it, and touch the dough. If it still feels sticky, add a little more flour, and process again until it is incorporated.

3 ▲ Remove the dough from the processor. Knead it for about 2–3 minutes on a surface dusted with the remaining flour. Form it into a ball. Proceed with Step 4 of Basic Pizza Dough.

Cheese and Tomato Pizza

Pizza alla Margherita

The Margherita is named after the nineteenth-century Queen of Italy, and is one of the most popular of all pizzas.

Ingredients

450 g/1 lb peeled plum tomatoes, fresh or canned, weighed whole, without extra juice
1 recipe Basic Pizza Dough, rolled out
350 g/12 oz/1¾ cups mozzarella cheese, cut into small dice
10–12 leaves fresh basil, torn into pieces
60 ml/4 tbsp freshly grated Parmesan cheese (optional)
salt and freshly ground black pepper
45 ml/3 tbsp olive oil
serves 4

1 Preheat the oven to 250°C/475°F/gas 9 for at least 20 minutes before baking. Strain the tomatoes through the medium holes of a food mill placed over a bowl, scraping in all the pulp.

2 ▲ Spread the puréed tomatoes onto the prepared pizza dough, leaving the rim uncovered.

3 ▲ Sprinkle evenly with the mozzarella. Dot with basil. Sprinkle with Parmesan if using, salt and pepper and olive oil. Immediately place the pizzas in the oven. Bake for about 15–20 minutes, or until the crust is golden brown and the cheeses are melted and bubbling.

Pizza with Mozzarella and Anchovies

Pizza alla napoletana

If you ask for a pizza in the Neapolitan manner anywhere in Italy other than in Naples, you will be given this pizza with anchovies.

Ingredients

450 g/1 lb peeled plum tomatoes, fresh or canned, weighed whole, without extra juice
1 recipe Basic Pizza Dough, rolled out
40 g/1½ oz/3 tbsp anchovy fillets in oil, drained and cut into pieces
350 g/12 oz/1¾ cups mozzarella cheese, cut into small dice
5 ml/1 tsp oregano leaves, fresh or dried
salt and freshly ground black pepper
45 ml/3 tbsp olive oil
serves 4

1 Preheat the oven to 250°C/475°F/gas 9 for at least 20 minutes before baking. Strain the tomatoes through the medium holes of a food mill placed over a bowl, scraping in all the pulp.

2 ▲ Spread the puréed tomatoes on the pizza dough, leaving the rim uncovered. Dot with the anchovy pieces and the mozzarella.

3 ▲ Sprinkle with oregano, salt and pepper, and olive oil. Immediately place the pizza in the oven. Bake for about 15–20 minutes, or until the crust is golden brown and the cheese is bubbling.

Four Seasons Pizza

Pizza quattro stagioni

The topping on this pizza is divided into four quarters, one for each "season". You may substitute suggested ingredients for any other seasonal favourites.

Ingredients

- 450 g/1 lb peeled plum tomatoes, fresh or canned, weighed whole, without extra juice
- 75 ml/5 tbsp olive oil
- 115 g/4 oz/1 cup mushrooms, thinly sliced
- 1 clove garlic, finely chopped
- 1 recipe Basic Pizza Dough, rolled out
- 350 g/12 oz/1¾ cups mozzarella cheese, cut into small dice
- 4 thin slices of ham, cut into 5 cm/2 in squares
- 32 black olives, stoned and halved
- 8 artichoke hearts preserved in oil, drained and cut in half
- 5 ml/1 tsp oregano leaves, fresh or dried
- salt and freshly ground black pepper

serves 4

1 ▲ Preheat the oven to 250°C/475°F/gas 9 for at least 20 minutes before baking the pizza. Strain the tomatoes through the medium holes of a food mill placed over a bowl, scraping in all the pulp.

2 Heat 30 ml/2 tbsp of the oil and lightly sauté the mushrooms. Stir in the garlic and set aside.

3 ▲ Spread the puréed tomato on the prepared pizza dough, leaving the rim uncovered. Sprinkle evenly with the mozzarella. Spread mushrooms over one quarter of each pizza.

4 ▲ Arrange the ham on another quarter, and the olives and artichoke hearts on the two remaining quarters. Sprinkle with oregano, salt and pepper, and the remaining olive oil. Immediately place the pizza in the oven. Bake for about 15–20 minutes, or until the crust is golden brown and the topping is bubbling.

Pizza with Fresh Vegetables

Pizza all'ortolana

This pizza can be made with any combination of fresh vegetables. Most will benefit from being blanched or sautéed before being baked on the pizza.

Ingredients

400 g/14 oz peeled plum tomatoes, fresh or canned, weighed whole, without extra juice
2 medium broccoli spears
225 g/8 oz fresh asparagus
2 small courgettes
75 ml/5 tbsp olive oil
50 g/2 oz/⅓ cup shelled peas, fresh or frozen
4 spring onions, sliced
1 recipe Basic Pizza Dough, rolled out
75 g/3 oz/½ cup mozzarella cheese, cut into small dice
10 leaves fresh basil, torn into pieces
2 cloves garlic, finely chopped
salt and freshly ground black pepper
serves 4

1 Preheat the oven to 250°C/475°F/gas 9 for at least 20 minutes before baking the pizza. Strain the tomatoes through the medium holes of a food mill placed over a bowl, scraping in all the pulp.

2 ▲ Peel the broccoli stems and asparagus, and blanch with the courgettes in a large pan of boiling water for 4–5 minutes. Drain. Cut into bite-size pieces.

3 Heat 30 ml/2 tbsp of the olive oil in a small pan. Stir in the peas and spring onions, and cook for 5–6 minutes, stirring often. Remove from the heat.

4 ▲ Spread the puréed tomatoes onto the pizza dough, leaving the rim uncovered. Add the other vegetables, spreading them evenly over the tomatoes.

5 ▲ Sprinkle with the mozzarella, basil, garlic, salt and pepper, and remaining olive oil. Immediately place the pizza in the oven. Bake for about 20 minutes, or until the crust is golden brown and the cheese has melted.

Pizza with Sausage

Pizza con salsicce

Use sausages with a high meat content for this topping.

Ingredients

450 g/1 lb peeled plum tomatoes, fresh or canned, weighed whole, without extra juice
1 recipe Basic Pizza Dough, rolled out
350 g/12 oz/1¾ cups mozzarella cheese, cut into small dice
225 g/8 oz/1½ cups sausage meat, removed from the casings and crumbled
5 ml/1 tsp oregano leaves, fresh or dried
salt and freshly ground black pepper
45 ml/3 tbsp olive oil
serves 4

1 Preheat the oven to 250°C/475°F/ gas 9 for at least 20 minutes before baking the pizza. Strain the tomatoes through the medium holes of a food mill placed over a bowl, scraping in all the pulp.

2 ▲ Spread some of the puréed tomatoes on the prepared pizza dough, leaving the rim uncovered. Sprinkle evenly with the mozzarella. Add the sausage meat in a layer.

3 ▲ Sprinkle with oregano, salt and pepper, and olive oil. Immediately place the pizza in the preheated oven. Bake for about 15–20 minutes, or until the crust is golden brown and the cheese is bubbling.

Pizza with Four Cheeses

Pizza con quattro formaggi

Any combination of cheeses can be used, but choose cheeses which are different in character.

Ingredients

1 recipe Basic Pizza Dough, rolled out
75 g/3 oz/½ cup Gorgonzola or other blue cheese, thinly sliced
75 g/3 oz/½ cup mozzarella cheese, finely diced
75 g/3 oz/½ cup goat's cheese, thinly sliced
75 g/3 oz/½ cup sharp Cheddar cheese, coarsely grated
4 leaves fresh sage, torn into pieces, or 45 ml/3 tbsp chopped fresh parsley
salt and freshly ground black pepper
45 ml/3 tbsp olive oil
serves 4

1 Preheat the oven to 250°C/475°F/ gas 9 for at least 20 minutes before baking the pizza. Arrange the Gorgonzola on one quarter of the pizza and the mozzarella on another, leaving the edge free.

2 ▲ Arrange the goat's and Cheddar cheeses on the remaining two quarters.

~ VARIATION ~

For an unusual taste, substitute 75 g/3 oz of sliced smoked cheese for one of the other cheeses.

3 ▲ Sprinkle with the herbs, salt and pepper, and olive oil. Immediately place the pizza in the oven. Bake for about 15–20 minutes, or until the crust is golden brown and the cheeses are bubbling.

Mediterranean Pizza

Pizza mediterranea

The combination of sweet and salty Mediterranean ingredients makes a delicious modern pizza topping.

Ingredients

12 sun-dried tomatoes, dry or in oil, drained
350 g/12 oz/1¾ cups goat's cheese, sliced as thinly as possible
1 recipe Basic Pizza Dough, rolled out
30 g/2 tbsp capers in brine or salt, rinsed
10 leaves fresh basil
salt and freshly ground black pepper
60 ml/4 tbsp olive oil
serves 4

1 Preheat the oven to 250°C/475°F/ gas 9 for at least 20 minutes before baking the pizza. Place the tomatoes in a small bowl, cover with hot water, and leave to soak for 15 minutes. Drain and cut into thin slices. (The soaking water may be saved to add to a pasta sauce or soup.)

2 ▲ Arrange the cheese on the prepared pizza dough in one layer, leaving the rim uncovered. Dot with the tomato slices.

3 ▲ Sprinkle with the capers and basil leaves. Allow to rise for 10 minutes before baking.

4 Sprinkle with salt, pepper and olive oil. Place the pizza in the oven. Bake for about 15–20 minutes, or until the crust is golden brown.

Pizza with Onions and Olives

Pizza con cipolle e olive

Onions cooked slowly to release their sweetness contrast with the salty bitterness of the olives.

Ingredients

90 ml/6 tbsp olive oil
4 medium onions, finely sliced
salt and freshly ground black pepper
1 recipe Basic Pizza Dough, rolled out
350 g/12 oz/1¾ cups mozzarella cheese, cut into small dice
32 black olives, stoned and halved
45 ml/3 tbsp chopped fresh parsley
serves 4

1 Preheat the oven to 250°C/475°F/ gas 9 for at least 20 minutes before baking the pizza. Heat half the oil in a large frying pan. Add the onions, and cook over low heat until soft, translucent, and beginning to brown, 12–15 minutes. Season with salt and pepper. Remove from the heat.

2 ▲ Spread the onions over the prepared pizza dough in an even layer, leaving the rim uncovered. Sprinkle with the mozzarella.

3 ▲ Dot with the olives. Sprinkle with parsley and the remaining olive oil. Immediately place the pizza in the oven. Bake for about 15–20 minutes, or until the crust is golden brown and the cheese is bubbling.

Pizza with Seafood

Pizza con frutti di mare

Any combination of shellfish or other seafood can be used as a pizza topping.

Ingredients

450 g/1 lb peeled plum tomatoes, fresh or canned, weighed whole, without extra juice
175 g/6 oz small squid
225 g/8 oz fresh mussels
1 recipe Basic Pizza Dough, rolled out
175 g/6 oz prawns, raw or cooked, peeled and deveined
2 cloves garlic, finely chopped
45 ml/3 tbsp chopped fresh parsley
salt and freshly ground black pepper
45 ml/3 tbsp olive oil
serves 4

1 ▲ Preheat the oven to 250°C/475°F/gas 9 for at least 20 minutes before baking the pizza. Strain the tomatoes through the medium holes of a food mill placed over a bowl, scraping in all the pulp.

2 ▲ Working near the sink, clean the squid by first peeling off the thin skin from the body section. Rinse well. Pull the head and tentacles away from the sac section. Some of the intestines will come away with the head.

3 ▲ Remove and discard the translucent quill and any remaining insides from the sac. Sever the tentacles from the head. Discard the head and intestines. Remove the small hard beak from the base of the tentacles. Rinse the sac and tentacles under running water. Drain. Slice the sacs into rings 5 mm/¼ in thick.

4 ▲ Scrape any barnacles off the mussels, and scrub well with a stiff brush. Rinse in several changes of cold water. Place the mussels in a saucepan and heat until they open. Lift them out with a slotted spoon, and remove to a side dish. (Discard any that do not open.) Break off the empty half shells, and discard.

5 ▲ Spread some of the puréed tomatoes on the prepared pizza dough, leaving the rim uncovered. Dot evenly with the prawns and squid rings and tentacles. Sprinkle with the garlic, parsley, salt and pepper, and olive oil. Immediately place the pizza in the oven. Bake for about 8 minutes.

6 ▲ Remove from the oven, and add the mussels in the half shells. Return to the oven and bake for 7–10 minutes more, or until the crust is golden.

~ VARIATION ~

Fresh clams may be added: scrub them well under cold running water. Place in a saucepan and heat until the shells open. Lift them out and remove to a side dish. Discard any that do not open. Break off the empty half shells, and discard. Add to the pizza after 8 minutes of baking.

Pizza with Herbs

Pizza in bianco con erbe aromatiche

This simple topping of mixed fresh herbs, olive oil and salt make a delicious hot pizza which can also be eaten as a bread. In Italy it is often served in a pizzeria and eaten as an appetizer.

Ingredients
1 recipe Basic Pizza Dough, rolled out
60 ml/4 tbsp chopped mixed fresh herbs such as thyme, rosemary, basil, parsley or sage
salt, to taste
90 ml/6 tbsp extra-virgin olive oil
serves 4

1 ▲ Preheat the oven to 250°C/475°F/ gas 9 for at least 20 minutes before baking the pizza. Sprinkle the prepared dough with the herbs, and salt.

2 ▲ Sprinkle with olive oil. Immediately place the pizza in the oven. Bake for about 20 minutes, or until the crust is golden brown.

Sicilian Closed Pizza

Sfinciuni

These exist in open and closed versions, and can be stuffed with any pizza topping.

Ingredients
1 recipe Basic Pizza Dough, risen once
30 ml/2 tbsp coarse cornmeal
3 hard-boiled eggs, peeled and sliced
50 g/2 oz/¼ cup anchovy fillets, drained and chopped
12 olives, stoned
8 leaves fresh basil, torn into pieces
6 medium tomatoes, peeled, seeded and diced
2 cloves garlic, finely chopped
freshly ground black pepper
175 g/6 oz/1½ cups grated caciocavallo or pecorino cheese
olive oil, for brushing
serves 4–6

1 Preheat the oven to 230°C/450°F/ gas 8. Punch the dough and knead lightly for 3–4 minutes. Divide the dough into two pieces, one slightly larger than the other. Lightly oil a round pizza pan 38 cm/15 inches in diameter. Sprinkle with the cornmeal. Roll or press the larger piece of dough into a round slightly bigger than the pan.

2 ▲ Transfer to the pan, bringing the dough up the sides of the pan to the rim. Fill the pie by placing the sliced eggs in the bottom in a layer, leaving the edges of the dough uncovered. Dot with the anchovies, olives and basil.

3 Spread the diced tomatoes over the other ingredients. Sprinkle with garlic and pepper. Top with the grated cheese.

4 ▲ Roll or press the other piece of dough into a circle the same size as the pan. Place it over the filling. Roll the edge of the bottom dough over it, and crimp together to make a border.

5 Brush the top and edges of the pie with olive oil. Bake for 30–40 minutes, or until the top is golden brown. Allow to stand for 5–8 minutes before slicing into wedges.

Calzone

Calzone

A calzone is a pizza folded over to enclose its filling. It can be made large or small, and stuffed with any of the flat pizza fillings. Calzoni can be eaten hot or cold.

Ingredients

1 recipe Basic Pizza Dough, risen once
350 g/12 oz/1½ cups ricotta cheese
175 g/6 oz/¾ cup ham, cut into small dice
6 medium tomatoes, peeled, seeded and diced
8 leaves fresh basil, torn into pieces
175 g/6 oz/1 cup mozzarella cheese, cut into small dice
60 ml/4 tbsp freshly grated Parmesan cheese
salt and freshly ground black pepper
olive oil, for brushing

serves 4

1 ▲ Preheat the oven to 250°C/475°F/gas 9 for at least 20 minutes before baking the calzoni. Punch the dough down and knead it lightly. Divide the dough into 4 balls.

2 ▲ Roll each ball out into a flat circle about 5 mm/¼ inch thick.

3 ▲ Combine all the filling ingredients in a bowl, and mix well. Season with salt and pepper.

4 ▲ Divide the filling between the 4 circles of dough, placing it on half of each circle and allowing a border of 2 cm/1 inch all around.

~ COOK'S TIP ~

The calzone is a speciality of Naples. Calzone means "trouser leg" in Italian. This pizza was so named because it resembled a leg of the baggy trousers worn by Neapolitan men in the 18th and 19th centuries. Calzoni are now usually round but were originally made from rectangular pieces of dough folded over a long central filling.

5 ▲ Fold the other half of the circle over. Crimp the edges of the dough together with your fingers to seal.

6 ▲ Place the calzoni on lightly oiled baking sheets. Brush the tops lightly with olive oil. Bake in the preheated oven for about 15–20 minutes, or until the tops are golden brown and the dough is puffed.

Focaccia

Focaccia

Focaccia is an antique form of flat bread which is oiled before baking. It is usually made in a large baking tray, and sold in bakeries cut into squares.

Ingredients
1 recipe Basic Pizza Dough, risen once
45 ml/3 tbsp olive oil
coarse sea salt
serves 6–8 as a side dish

1 ▲ After punching the dough down, knead it for 3–4 minutes. Brush a large shallow baking pan with 15 ml/1 tbsp of the oil.

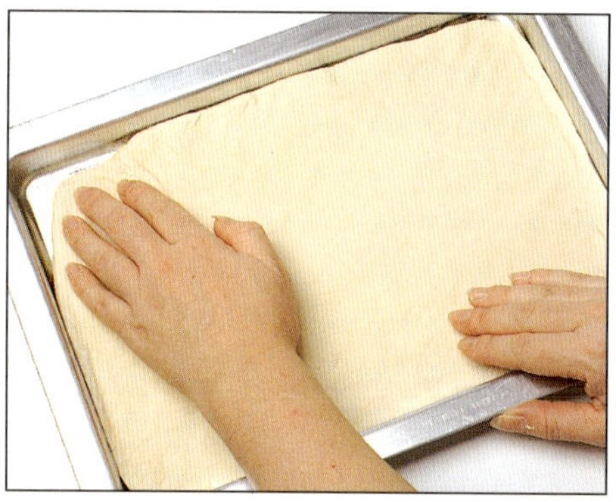

2 ▲ Place the dough in the pan, and use your fingers to press it into an even layer 2 cm/1 inch thick. Cover the dough with a cloth, and leave to rise in a warm place for 30 minutes. Preheat the oven to 200°C/400°F/gas 6.

~ COOK'S TIP ~

To freeze, allow to cool to room temperature after baking. Wrap in foil and freeze. Thaw and place in a warm oven before serving.

3 ▲ Just before baking, use your fingers to press rows of light indentations into the surface of the focaccia dough.

4 ▲ Brush with the remaining oil, and sprinkle lightly with coarse salt. Bake for about 25 minutes, or until just golden. Cut into squares or wedges and serve as an accompaniment to a meal, or alone, warm or at room temperature.

Focaccia with Onions

Focaccia con cipolle

This appetizing flat bread has a topping of sautéed onions. It can be split and filled with prosciutto or cheese for an unusual sandwich.

Ingredients
1 recipe Basic Pizza Dough, risen once
75 ml/5 tbsp olive oil
1 medium onion, sliced very thinly and cut into short lengths
½ tsp fresh thyme leaves
coarse sea salt
serves 6–8 as a side dish

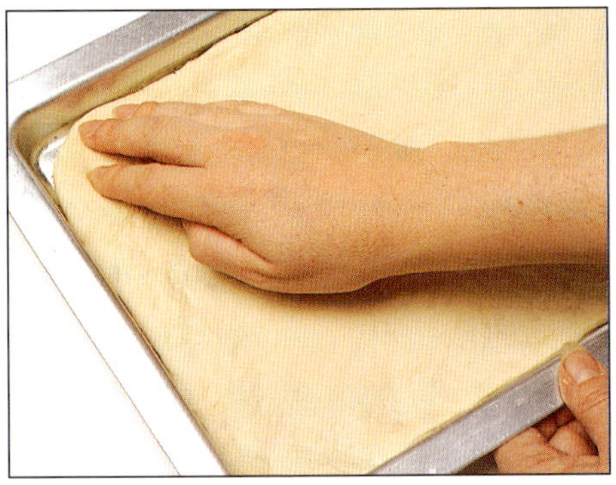

1 ▲ After punching the dough down, knead it for 3–4 minutes. Brush a large shallow baking pan with 15 ml/1 tbsp of the oil. Place the dough in the pan, and use your fingers to press it into an even layer 2 cm/1 inch thick. Cover the dough with a cloth, and leave to rise in a warm place for 30 minutes. Preheat the oven to 200°C/400°F/gas 6 for 30 minutes during this time.

2 ▲ While the focaccia is rising, heat 45 ml/3 tbsp of the oil in a medium frying pan. Add the onion, and cook over low heat until soft. Stir in the thyme.

3 ▲ Just before baking, use your fingers to press rows of light indentations into the surface of the focaccia. Brush with the remaining oil.

4 ▲ Spread the onions evenly over the top, and sprinkle lightly with coarse salt. Bake for about 25 minutes, or until just golden. Cut into squares or wedges and serve as an accompaniment to a meal, or alone, warm or at room temperature.

Focaccia with Olives

Focaccia con olive

For this topping, pieces of stoned green olives are pressed onto the dough before baking.

Ingredients
1 recipe Basic Pizza Dough, risen once
45 ml/3 tbsp olive oil
10–12 large green olives, stoned and cut in half lengthwise
coarse sea salt
serves 6–8 as a side dish

1 After punching the dough down, knead it for 3–4 minutes. Brush a large shallow baking pan with 15 ml/1 tbsp of the oil. Place the dough in the pan, and use your fingers to press it into an even layer 2 cm/1 inch thick. Cover the dough with a cloth, and leave to rise in a warm place for 30 minutes. Preheat the oven to 200°C/400°F/gas 6 for 30 minutes during this time.

2 ▲ Just before baking, use your fingers to press rows of light indentations into the surface of the focaccia. Brush with the remaining oil.

3 ▲ Dot evenly with the olive pieces, and sprinkle with a little coarse salt. Bake for about 25 minutes, or until just golden. Cut into squares or wedges and serve as an accompaniment to a meal, or alone, warm or at room temperature.

Focaccia with Rosemary

Focaccia con rosmarino

One of the most popular breads. If possible, use fresh rosemary for this recipe.

Ingredients
1 recipe Basic Pizza Dough, risen once
45 ml/3 tbsp olive oil
2 medium sprigs fresh rosemary, coarse stalks removed
coarse sea salt
serves 6–8 as a side dish

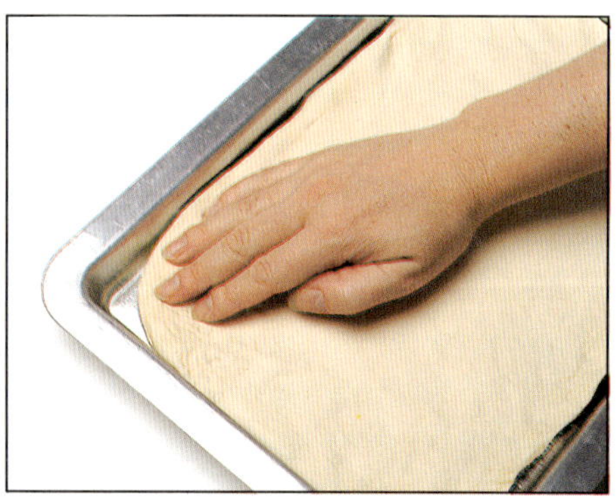

1 ▲ After punching the dough down, knead it for 3–4 minutes. Brush a large shallow baking pan with 15 ml/1 tbsp of the oil. Place the dough in the pan, and use your fingers to press it into an even layer 2 cm/1 inch thick.

2 ▲ Scatter with the rosemary leaves. Cover the dough with a cloth, and leave to rise in a warm place for 30 minutes. Preheat the oven to 200°C/400°F/gas 6 for 30 minutes during this time.

3 ▲ Just before baking, use your fingers to press rows of light indentations into the surface of the focaccia. Brush with the remaining oil, and sprinkle lightly with coarse salt. Bake for about 25 minutes, or until just golden. Cut into squares or wedges and serve as an accompaniment to a meal, or alone, warm or at room temperature.

Italian Bread Sticks

Grissini

These typically Italian bread sticks are especially delicious when hand-made. They are still sold loose in many bakeries in Turin and the north of Italy.

Ingredients

15 g/½ oz/1 tbsp fresh cake yeast or 7 g/¼ oz/½ tbsp active dried yeast
100 ml/4 fl oz/½ cup lukewarm water
pinch sugar
10 ml/2 tsp malt extract (optional)
5 ml/1 tsp salt
200–225 g/7–8 oz/1¾–2 cups plain flour
makes about 30

1 ▲ Warm a medium mixing bowl by swirling some hot water in it. Drain. Place the yeast in the bowl, and pour on the warm water. Stir in the sugar, mix with a fork, and allow to stand until the yeast has dissolved and starts to foam, 5–10 minutes.

2 ▲ Use a wooden spoon to mix in the malt extract, if using, the salt and about one-third of the flour. Mix in another third of the flour, stirring with the spoon until the dough forms a mass and begins to pull away from the sides of the bowl.

3 ▲ Sprinkle some of the remaining flour onto a smooth work surface. Remove all of the dough from the bowl, and begin to knead it, working in the remaining flour a little at a time. Knead for 8–10 minutes. By the end the dough should be elastic and smooth. Form it into a ball.

4 ▲ Tear a lump the size of a small walnut from the ball of dough. Róll it lightly between your hands into a small sausage shape. Set it aside on a lightly floured surface. Repeat until all the dough is used up. There should be about 30 pieces.

~ VARIATION ~

Grissini are also good when rolled lightly in poppy or sesame seeds before being baked.

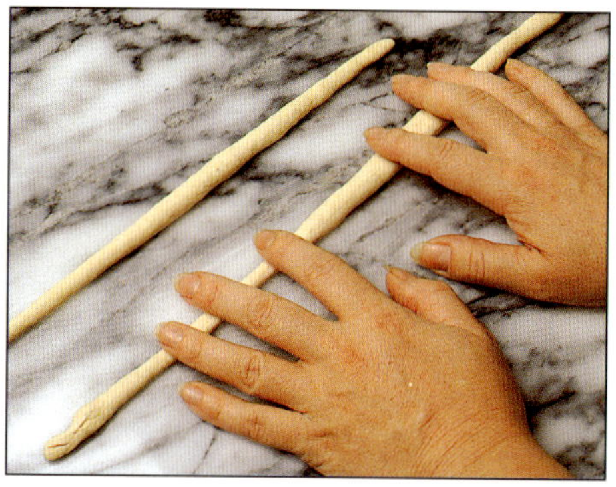

5 ▲ Place one piece of dough on a clean smooth work surface without any flour on it. Roll the dough under the spread-out fingers of both hands, moving your hands backwards and forwards to lengthen and thin the dough into a long strand about 1 cm/⅜ inch thick. Transfer to a very lightly greased baking tray. Repeat with the remaining dough pieces, taking care to roll all the grissini to about the same thickness.

6 ▲ Preheat the oven to 200°C/400°F/gas 6. Cover the tray with a cloth, and place the grissini in a warm place to rise for 10–15 minutes while the oven is heating. Bake for about 8–10 minutes. Remove from the oven. Turn the grissini over, and return them to the oven for 6–7 minutes more. Do not let them brown. Allow to cool. Grissini should be crisp when served. If they lose their crispness on a damp day, warm them in a moderate oven for a few minutes before serving.

Bread with Grapes

Schiacciata con uva

This bread is made to celebrate the grape harvest in central Italy. Use small black grapes with or without seeds; in Italy wine grapes are used.

Ingredients
750 g/1½ lb small black grapes
115 g/4 oz/½ cup sugar
1 recipe Basic Pizza Dough, risen once
30 ml/2 tbsp olive oil
serves 6–8

1 ▲ Remove the grapes from the stems. Wash them well, and pat dry with paper towels. Place in a bowl and sprinkle with the sugar. Set aside until they are needed.

2 ▲ Knead the dough lightly. Divide it into two halves. Roll out or press one half into a circle about 1 cm/½ inch thick. Place on a lightly oiled flat baking sheet. Sprinkle with half of the sugared grapes.

3 ▲ Roll out or press the second half of the dough into a circle the same size as the first. Place it on top of the first.

4 ▲ Crimp the edges together. Sprinkle the top with the remaining grapes. Cover the dough with a dish towel and leave in a warm place to rise for 30 minutes. Preheat the oven to 190°C/375°F/gas 5. Sprinkle the bread with the oil, and bake for 50–60 minutes. Allow to cool before cutting into wedges.

Tomato and Basil Tart

Torta di pomodoro e basilico

This tart is similar to a pizza, but uses shortcrust pastry instead of yeast dough for the base.

Ingredients

175 g/6 oz/1½ cups flour
½ tsp salt, plus more to sprinkle
115 g/4 oz/½ cup butter or margarine, chilled
45–75 ml/3–5 tbsp cold water
30 ml/2 tbsp extra-virgin olive oil

For the filling

175 g/6 oz/1 cup mozzarella cheese, sliced as thinly as possible
12 leaves fresh basil
4–5 medium tomatoes, cut into 5 mm/¼ in slices
salt and freshly ground black pepper
60 ml/4 tbsp freshly grated Parmesan cheese

serves 6–8

1 ▲ Make the pastry by placing the flour and salt in a mixing bowl. Using a pastry blender, cut the butter or margarine into the dry ingredients until the mixture resembles coarse meal. Add 45 ml/3 tbsp of water, and combine with a fork until the dough holds together. If it is too crumbly, mix in a little more water.

2 Gather the dough into a ball and flatten it into a disc. Wrap in greaseproof paper and refrigerate for at least 40 minutes. Preheat the oven to 190°C/375°F/gas 5.

3 Roll the pastry out between two sheets of greaseproof paper to a thickness of 5 mm/¼ inch. Line a 28 cm/11 inch tart or pie pan, trimming the edges evenly. Refrigerate for 20 minutes. Prick the bottom all over with a fork.

4 ▲ Line the pastry with a sheet of baking parchment. Fill with dried beans. Place the pie pan on a baking tray and bake about 15 minutes. Remove from the oven. Leave the oven on.

5 Remove the beans and paper. Brush the pastry with oil. Line with the mozzarella. Tear half of the basil into pieces, and sprinkle on top.

6 ▲ Arrange the tomato slices over the cheese. Dot with the remaining whole basil leaves. Sprinkle with salt and pepper, Parmesan and oil. Bake for about 35 minutes. If the cheese exudes a lot of liquid during baking, tilt the pan and spoon it off to keep the pastry from becoming soggy. Serve hot or at room temperature.

Potato Pizza

Pizza di patate

This "pizza" made of mashed potatoes, with a filling of anchovies, capers and tomatoes, is a speciality of Puglia.

Ingredients
1 kg/2 lb potatoes, scrubbed
100 ml/4 fl oz/½ cup extra-virgin olive oil
salt and freshly ground black pepper
2 cloves garlic, finely chopped
350 g/12 oz tomatoes, diced
3 anchovy fillets, chopped
30 ml/2 tbsp capers, rinsed
serves 4

1 ▲ Boil the potatoes in their skins until tender. Peel and mash or pass through a food mill. Beat in 45 ml/3 tbsp of the oil, and season.

2 Heat another 45 ml/3 tbsp of the oil in a medium saucepan. Add the garlic and the chopped tomatoes, and cook over moderate heat until the tomatoes soften and begin to dry out, 12–15 minutes. Meanwhile, preheat the oven to 200°C/400°F/gas 6.

3 ▲ Oil a shallow baking dish. Spread half the mashed potatoes into the dish in an even layer. Cover with the tomatoes, and dot with the chopped anchovies and the capers.

4 ▲ Spread the rest of the potatoes in a layer on top of the filling. Brush the top with the remaining oil. Bake in the preheated oven for 20–25 minutes, or until the top is golden brown.

~ VARIATION ~

For a vegetarian version of this dish, omit the anchovies. A few stoned and chopped olives may be added to the filling instead.

Bruschetta with Tomato

Bruschetta con pomodoro

Bruschetta is toasted or grilled bread, rubbed with garlic and sprinkled with olive oil or chopped fresh tomatoes. It is eaten as an appetizer or accompaniment.

Ingredients
3–4 medium tomatoes, chopped
salt and freshly ground black pepper
a few leaves fresh basil, torn into pieces
8 slices crusty white bread
2–3 cloves garlic, peeled and cut in half
90 ml/6 tbsp extra-virgin olive oil
serves 4

1 Place the chopped tomatoes with their juice in a small bowl. Season with salt and pepper, and stir in the basil. Allow to stand for 10 minutes.

2 ▲ Toast or grill the bread until it is crisp on both sides. Rub one side of each piece of toast with the cut garlic.

3 ▲ Arrange on a platter. Sprinkle with the olive oil. Spoon on the chopped tomatoes, and serve at once.

Crostini with Cheese

Crostini con formaggio

Crostini are small pieces of toasted bread. They can be made with various toppings, and are served hot or cold with drinks. This cheese-topped version is always popular.

Ingredients

4–6 slices day-old white or brown bread
75 g/3 oz/¾ cup thinly sliced cheese (fontina, Cheddar or gruyère)
anchovy fillets
strips of grilled red pepper
freshly ground black pepper
serves 6

1 ▲ Cut the bread into small shapes (triangle, circle, oval, etc.). Preheat the oven to 190°C/375°F/gas 5.

2 ▲ Place a thin slice of cheese on each piece of bread, cutting it to fit.

3 ▲ Cut the anchovy fillets and strips of pepper into small decorative shapes and place on top of the cheese. Grind a little pepper on each.

4 ▲ Butter a baking sheet. Place the crostini on it, and bake for 10 minutes, or until the cheese has melted. Serve straight from the oven, or allow to cool before serving.

~ VARIATION ~

For a colourful addition use strips of green or yellow pepper.

Crostini with Mussels or Clams

Crostini con cozze o vongole

Each of these seafood crostini is topped with a mussel or clam, and then baked. This recipe comes from Genoa. Use fresh seafood whenever possible.

Ingredients
16 large mussels or clams, in their shells
4 large slices bread, 2.5 cm/1 in thick
40 g/1½ oz/3 tbsp butter
30 ml/2 tbsp chopped fresh parsley
1 shallot, very finely chopped
olive oil, for brushing
lemon sections, to serve
makes 16

1 ▲ Wash the mussels or clams well in several changes of water. Cut the "beards" off the mussels. Place the shellfish in a saucepan with a cupful of water, and heat until the shells open. (Discard any that do not open.) As soon as they open, lift the molluscs out of the pan. Spoon out of their shells, and set aside. Preheat the oven to 190°C/375°F/gas 5.

2 ▲ Cut the crusts off the bread. Cut each slice into quarters. Scoop out a hollow from the top of each piece large enough to hold a mussel or clam. Do not cut through to the bottom.

3 ▲ Break the scooped-out bread into crumbs, and reserve. In a small frying pan, heat the butter. Cook the parsley with the shallot and the breadcrumbs until the shallot softens.

4 ▲ Brush each piece of bread with olive oil. Place one mussel or clam in each hollow. Spoon a small amount of the parsley and shallot mixture onto each mollusc. Place on an oiled baking sheet. Bake for 10 minutes. Serve at once, while still hot, with the lemon sections.

INDEX